Prologue

I pray that this book will serve as a useful tool in the practical aspects of the Christian life, and that it will bring light concerning our conflict with the forces of evil and unclean spirits—exposing some of the many strategies they use to influence our lives. May the God of peace bless you abundantly and make you a thousand times more than you are today.

Table of Contents

Chapter 1
Angels as Ministers to the Heirs of Salvation

Every system of government rests on three foundational pillars through which it exercises authority: the executive branch, the legislative branch, and the judicial branch. The executive branch is responsible for enforcing the law; the legislative branch is tasked with creating the laws needed to govern; and the judicial branch is charged with interpreting the law and administering justice. In democratic nations, these powers are kept separate to ensure balance within the government.

The Kingdom of Heaven, as a universal government, is not lacking in these three pillars. Within the heavenly government, we also find the executive, legislative, and judicial powers.

The legislative power of the Kingdom of Heaven is the Word of God: "For the Lord is our judge, the Lord is our lawgiver, the Lord is our king; he will save us" (Isaiah 33:22). This Word has been established from eternity: "He hath also stablished them for ever and ever: he hath made a decree which shall not pass" (Psalm 148:6). By it, all of creation is governed; it endures forever and is unchanging. It is the supreme standard by which justice is executed, behavior is guided, and the measure by which we will be judged is revealed (John 12:48).

There is no need to amend it, for it has been perfect from the beginning; it contains neither error nor deficiency. It is from eternity to eternity, without variation of any kind, which guarantees firmness in the manner of governance. Otherwise, we would have no assurance for the years to come.

If the law of the Kingdom of Heaven were subject to change, what guarantee would we have that our salvation is eternal and immutable in nature? But thanks be to God that, though heaven and earth shall pass away, His Word shall not pass away. This is something we must understand clearly, for the authority given to the Church in Christ Jesus is grounded in the legislative power—that is, in the Word of God. The fact that the Word is eternal and unchanging guarantees us an eternal and unchanging Kingdom.

This system of laws, ordinances, and decrees—which we know as the legislative power—has been revealed to mankind through the Bible, also called the Scriptures. From the book of Genesis to the book of Revelation, the constitution of the Kingdom of Heaven has been made known to humankind.

The Christian, as a citizen of God's Kingdom, is called to know this constitution—the Word of God—if he truly desires to be effective in his role as one who governs.

From a functional perspective, the executive and judicial powers rest upon the legislative power—that is, upon the Word of God. The legislative power is the normative foundation upon which the roles of the executive and the judiciary are based, since neither can legitimately act outside the framework of the law.

The Kingdom of Heaven will not issue a judgment that is not backed by the Scriptures, nor will the executive power issue a decree without a legal foundation. Therefore, knowing the Scriptures is indispensable for all who are part of God's Kingdom, for every executive command and every judgment must be based on the Word of God.

The judicial power is responsible for executing judgment. In the Kingdom of Heaven, judgment has been entrusted to Christ: "For the Father judgeth no man, but hath committed all judgment unto the Son" (John 5:22).

And Christ, as the executor of justice, consists of the Lord Jesus, who is the Head, and the Church, which is His body: "For the husband is the head of the wife, even as Christ is the head of the church: and he is the saviour of the body" (Ephesians 5:23).

Therefore, justice in the Kingdom of Heaven is administered by the Lord Jesus and by each one who is part of the body of Christ: "Know ye not that we shall judge angels? how much more things that pertain to this life?" (1 Corinthians 6:3).

It is worth noting that, as judges, a thorough knowledge of the law is of utmost importance, especially considering that, as members of the body of Christ, we have a role within the judicial authority. It would be highly irresponsible to render judgment without understanding the Scriptures.

Perhaps this is the reason why many believers today are unfit to judge—for the Kingdom of Heaven will not allow a believer to execute judgment while ignorant of the legislative power. It would be an act of gross irresponsibility.

Imagine, for a moment, a judge of the republic who is unfamiliar with the law. How would such a judge pronounce a sentence? How could anyone trust his judgment? The State would be obligated to suspend or remove him from office.

This is the case for many believers today: they have been suspended from judgment due to their incompetence, as their Bibles remain open only to Psalm 91, day and night, waiting for someone to pick them up and study them.

Revelation 20:4 reveals that only those who had been given authority to judge were seated on the thrones

John saw. It seems not everyone has been granted this authority, and the primary reason is a lack of knowledge of the Scriptures.

Therefore, before we even begin to talk about angels, it is important to pause and responsibly consider how seriously we take the Scriptures.

How many years of their lives do earthly judges invest in order to practice their profession? If this is the standard in matters of this world, how much more seriousness should a child of God show when it comes to their knowledge of the Scriptures?

Such was the case in the church of Corinth, to the point that the apostle Paul was compelled to rebuke them and remind them that they were called to judge the world—and even the angels (1 Corinthians 6:2–3). Yet they were unable to resolve even trivial disputes among themselves. This was the result of their inability to understand the Scriptures.

In summary, the judicial power belongs to Christ and the Church, and it is founded upon the legislative power—that is, the Scriptures. Without the Scriptures, there is no judgment, for "where no law is, there is no transgression" (Romans 5:13). Therefore, anyone who desires to participate in judgment must undoubtedly have knowledge of the Word of God.

Lastly, we come to the executive power, which is exercised by the appropriate authorities. In democratic nations, this power is represented by the president, governors, or mayors, along with their respective ministers or secretaries. It is their responsibility to enforce the law throughout the national territory by means of public force.

It is crucial that, when an executive order is issued, it originates from a legitimate authority; otherwise, it has no validity or power.

The individual must be invested with the necessary authority to issue an executive order—this is not something just anyone can do. In a democracy, the person authorized and empowered to issue such a decree is the president. He holds the authority granted by the state.

In the Kingdom of Heaven, the ones entrusted with exercising the executive power are those who possess a kingdom, for issuing such orders is the role of kings.

"And hast made us unto our God kings and priests: and we shall reign on the earth" (Revelation 5:10). This biblical declaration testifies to the royalty granted to the people of God, which is His Church. Thus, as the Church, every member of the body of Christ is authorized to issue executive orders, for those who have obeyed the gospel have been seated with Christ in heavenly places—and Christ is exalted above angels, authorities, and powers.

"Who is gone into heaven, and is on the right hand of God; angels and authorities and powers being made subject unto him" (1 Peter 3:22). And by being seated with Christ, Christians partake of this authority, which enables them to issue executive orders within the scope of the Kingdom of Heaven.

It is vital to grow in the knowledge and revelation of the authority we possess through our union with Christ, because ignorance of that authority leads to negligence in the responsibilities that come with it.

Authority is not an ornament in the life of the believer—it carries a demand:

"But he that knew not, and did commit things worthy of stripes, shall be beaten with few stripes. For unto whomsoever much is given, of him shall be much required: and to whom men have committed much, of him they will ask the more" (Luke 12:48).

The one who has been given authority is responsible for exercising the power it grants, to ensure the protection of those under his care. Therefore, a Christian who does not diligently grow in the knowledge of this authority is not only negligent but also irresponsible—because by failing to use it, he may leave unprotected all that has been entrusted to him.

We cannot blame God for situations that result from the neglect of authority. In fact, the failure to use authority can be more damaging than its misuse, because neglect gives the adversary freedom to invade a given jurisdiction. When an authority is careless and irresponsible, its enemies are strengthened, and its territory becomes overrun with trouble. Thus, it is not wise to hide behind ignorance as a justification for failing to exercise the authority that the Christian has received through union with Christ.

Having discussed the primary sources of governmental authority, let us now briefly examine the enforcement arm of that authority—because power and authority are not the same. Believers may not be strong in force, but they do have authority:

"Behold, I give unto you power to tread on serpents and scorpions, and over all the power of the enemy: and nothing shall by any means hurt you" (Luke 10:19).

When a government issues an executive or judicial order, there must be an enforcing force—otherwise, rebellion would prevail, and no government could stand. Earthly governments have their enforcement branches, also known as public forces, composed of various police departments and military forces at different levels. These are the ones tasked with enforcing the orders issued by the proper authorities.

The Kingdom of Heaven is no exception in this regard; it also has a heavenly enforcement force responsible for carrying out the commands issued by Kingdom authorities. These are the angels:

"Bless the Lord, ye his angels, that excel in strength, that do his commandments, hearkening unto the voice of his word" (Psalm 103:20).

When speaking of angels, the Word of God tells us that they excel in strength and do his commandments, hearkening unto the voice of his word. This reveals their function in the Kingdom of God.

They have been equipped with strength; and strength is essential to every government—for without it, rebellion could not be punished. Therefore, God's Kingdom has a force not only prepared to suppress rebellion but also attentive to the voice of God's command, ready to execute it promptly.

Among angels, there are different ranks and levels of strength. So, depending on the nature of the situation, the heavenly host is deployed accordingly. And since Christians have been seated with Christ in heavenly places, we can understand that the authority of the believer is greater than that of angels:

"Are they not all ministering spirits, sent forth to minister for them who shall be heirs of salvation?" (Hebrews 1:14).

It is important to emphasize that angels are attentive to the voice of the command. For this command to be carried out by the angels, two basic requirements must be met:

1. It must be fully grounded in the legislative power—that is, in the Word of God.

2. It must be issued by a competent authority—that is, by someone who possesses governmental authority within the Kingdom of God.

Although the Christian has the necessary authority in Christ to issue such commands, it is imperative to emphasize the need for knowledge of divine law; for angels will not execute a command that lacks foundation in the Scriptures. For this reason, the Christian, as an authority within the Kingdom, must be fully aligned with the Word of God.

Many of God's children have suffered unnecessary afflictions and hardships because they lack understanding of how the Kingdom of Heaven operates. At times, we expect the Kingdom to intervene on our behalf, when in reality, the Kingdom is waiting for the believer to issue an order—according to the divine command—so that the heavenly forces may be released to carry it out.

We must not receive every form of suffering that comes into our lives passively, without first discerning the spiritual reality we are facing. In many cases, it is indeed necessary for the believer to endure various tribulations:

"Confirming the souls of the disciples, and exhorting them to continue in the faith, and that we must through much tribulation enter into the kingdom of God" (Acts 14:22).

But there are also many situations in which suffering was not strictly necessary.

Faith plays a crucial role in all of this. Let us remember that angels obey the voice of the Lord's command—and that command is the Word of God. So, if suffering arises or is triggered by something contrary to the Word, then we are responsible for putting an end to that suffering.

For example, many mental struggles begin with internal words—depression, self-pity, frustration, anxiety, and so on. These can lead to very serious illnesses. However, we cannot passively accept such suffering, since these conditions often originate in thought patterns that go against the Word of God.

For instance, if a believer starts to experience anxious thoughts and gradually gives in to them, he may begin to suffer from overactivation of the nervous system, which can disrupt neurotransmitters and lead to symptoms such as tension, insomnia, and irrational thoughts. Over time, this may affect memory, judgment, and emotional stability.

But if instead, he exercises his authority and declares the Word—which is the law of the Kingdom of God:

"Casting all your care upon him; for he careth for you" (1 Peter 5:7),

—and changes his posture based on that Word—then the force of the Kingdom of Heaven will immediately come to his defense. Grounded in what the law of the Kingdom says, the believer can issue an executive order, administrative command, or decree to counter the attack of evil spirits. Such an order might be something like:

"In the name of Jesus, I silence every evil spirit seeking to fill my heart with anxiety."

This command is grounded in a Kingdom precept (1 Peter 5:7), and because of that, God's angels will immediately respond to it, silencing those spiritual forces.

As children of God, we have at our service the deployment of whatever heavenly troops are necessary in our battle against darkness. It is essential that, by faith, we exercise the authority granted to us in Christ in order for this to be activated.

In the midst of conflict, many believers simply remain silent—and this is extremely harmful, because silence can be a form of consent.

Evil spirits require human agreement with their lies in order to manifest that reality in a person's life. And that permission is often granted through silence. For example, if a believer senses thoughts such as "you don't matter to anyone" or "you're completely alone," and says nothing in response, the evil spirits will interpret that silence as approval. But if, on the contrary, the believer exercises his authority and invokes the divine constitution—that is, the Word of God—and says:

"For he hath said, I will never leave thee, nor forsake thee" (Hebrews 13:5),

that declaration, when spoken by an executive authority of the Kingdom of Heaven, sets heavenly forces in motion on his behalf.

The Lord Jesus Christ taught us this principle when He resisted Satan's lies in the wilderness. Every time Satan attempted to deceive Him, the Lord responded by declaring the constitution of the Kingdom of Heaven, saying, "It is written." And after these things, the Bible says:

"Then the devil leaveth him, and, behold, angels came and ministered unto him" (Matthew 4:11).

In the same way, whenever a child of God makes use of the Word, the public force of the Kingdom is dispatched to serve him.

The forces of evil will take advantage of passivity to launch even stronger attacks. In warfare, it is crucial to exercise authority—and we do this by declaring the Word of God. Therefore, remaining silent is equivalent to empowering the enemy and rendering the angels unable to assist us. But why is silence so dangerous in these cases? It's not that silence itself is wrong; the problem is not knowing when to be silent and when to speak. And this requires knowledge of the Word of God and prayer— these two work together to give us revelation.

On the night the Lord was arrested, He revealed this principle to Peter when He said: "Thinkest thou that I cannot now pray to my Father, and he shall presently give me more than twelve legions of angels?" (Matthew 26:53). This event reveals two key principles concerning spiritual warfare.

First principle: As a child of God, the believer has the right to ask the Father for whatever military force is necessary for their defense. This means our battles are executed by forces outside of ourselves—in other words, the angels are the ones who confront the forces of darkness directly. However, the believer is the one responsible for administering the battle because of his position of authority. The faith of the believer in the Word of God is expressed through words, actions, and even gestures. All of these send a message into the spiritual realm that can determine the outcome of the battle.

Spiritual maturity in warfare is closely tied to understanding this. Consider the example of Moses on the mountain: every time he lowered his hands, Amalek prevailed. I must stress the importance of grasping this principle, because some believers assume that good must always prevail, regardless of our efforts. However, Scripture shows us that evil can triumph when the conflict is mismanaged.

Had Moses continued in fatigue and left his hands lowered, Amalek would likely have defeated the people. Thus, the administration of the conflict led by Moses was essential. The victory did not depend on Joshua's strength in the valley, but on the signal received by the angels in the heavens. This was not merely a battle of men, but a spiritual conflict administered by men.

The military force the Kingdom was deploying at that moment was being regulated by the signal Moses gave with his hands. In that sense, Moses was the administrator of the war. Likewise, the believer administers the battle—and the angels fight it. The final outcome is determined by the believer's faith. As the apostle John said: "And this is the victory that overcometh the world, even our faith" (1 John 5:4). Faith demonstrates our conviction in the Word of God and can be expressed in many ways. The most important factor in any spiritual battle is the manifestation of faith, for it testifies that the believer trusts in the constitution of the Kingdom of Heaven—that is, the Word of God. In Moses' case, his faith was demonstrated by keeping his hands raised.

The information we transmit during the conflict is critical. Angels receive the signal of our faith through our words, attitudes, gestures, or actions. Therefore, it is important to reflect on how our faith is being manifested. Otherwise, we may hinder the work that the Kingdom of Heaven seeks to carry out in our favor through the angels.

Often, angels are simply waiting for a word of faith to be released by an executive authority of the Kingdom of Heaven in order to act—but that word is never spoken.

In many of our conflicts, it is essential to declare words of authority grounded in the legislative power of the Kingdom—that is, in the Word of God. Without the proclamation or confession of that Word, angels have no authority to act.

Several years ago, while visiting a city, I was approached by two men. They told me not to scream or run, threatening to take my life if I did. Their intention was to rob me of the money I was carrying.

Faced with this situation, and a bit nervous, I declared a word of authority in the name of the Lord Jesus Christ. Immediately, these men literally stepped back, as if someone had pushed them, and they walked away without a word.

Seen from a spiritual perspective, it was the command I issued that authorized my immediate defense, causing the angel assigned to me to act with the necessary force for my protection. Had I remained silent, it's very likely they would have robbed and assaulted me.

So, it is not wise to simply sit and cry when the enemy assaults us. At times, like spiritual infants, we blame God for the devil's attacks—attacks that were only possible due to our failure to use the authority we have received in Christ Jesus.

Imagine a mayor or local official who has been assigned responsibility over a certain district. Instead of taking action, he complains to his superiors and blames them for the rise in crime within his jurisdiction.

Clearly, such a person should be removed from office, for the very reason he was given authority was to maintain order in that territory. If that order is not being maintained, the fault lies solely with him.

In the same way, the Christian has been seated with Christ in heavenly places. This is not a light or symbolic authority—it is real and powerful. It is unworthy of a child of God to constantly weep over Satan's attacks. Spiritual maturity in warfare means understanding this principle clearly.

The Lord said to Moses: "Wherefore criest thou unto me? speak unto the children of Israel, that they go forward" (Exodus 14:15). When it comes to exercising authority, the issue is not to cry out—the issue is to speak.

The enemy has taken advantage of this confusion to plunder many believers. And what's worse is that this plundering is endured without any resistance.

It is important to understand that angels, as the enforcement force of the executive power of the Kingdom of Heaven, are attentive to the voice of the divine command, which is issued by the authorities of the Kingdom—that is, the children of God.

Second Principle: Twelve Legions

A Roman legion was composed of four to six thousand men. If we take the higher number—six thousand angels per legion—that means the Lord referred to seventy-two thousand angels available for His defense.

At first glance, one might think the Lord was exaggerating in asking for such a vast heavenly force, especially considering that a single angel killed one hundred and eighty-five thousand Assyrians in a single night (2 Kings 19:35).

Now imagine what seventy-two thousand could do. And yet, within this statement lies a deeper spiritual principle.

The primary force of the kingdom of darkness is also composed of angels—fallen angels, to be specific (Revelation 12:7). Therefore, the same framework of power that applies to the angels of God also operates, by nature, in the fallen angels. Though they have fallen morally, this does not mean they have lost their power, since power is intrinsic to their nature.

What the Kingdom of Heaven does is not to remove their power, but rather to strip them of authority by subjecting them to eternal judgment. Among fallen angels, there are also princes, rulers, and powers:

"For we wrestle not against flesh and blood, but against principalities, against powers, against the rulers of the darkness of this world, against spiritual wickedness in high places" (Ephesians 6:12).

For this reason, certain battles require a specific number of troops. Understanding this truth would greatly help us in the spiritual warfare we face daily. We should not assume that a single angel is always sufficient to defend us against all the arsenal of hell. If that were the case, the Lord would not have spoken of seventy-two thousand angels available for His defense on the night of Gethsemane.

This relates to the ranks of power and authority among angels themselves. If the angel of the Lord assigned to a believer is of lesser strength than the dark angel opposing him, he will need reinforcements from Heaven—a superior force—for protection.

The Lord Jesus mentioned seventy-two thousand angels because of the immense spiritual force that Satan unleashed against Him that night. Of course, the Lord only said He could ask for that number—He never actually did, because the divine purpose was to go to the cross. Still, the mention of that number is significant.

This was not about the small group of men who came with Judas. It was about the vast army Satan led that night, seeking to cut the Lord off from the land of the living. To counter such a force, seventy-two thousand war angels would have been necessary to prevent His arrest.

We see this principle also in 2 Kings 6:17. Elisha was surrounded by the Syrian army, who clearly had evil intentions. Elisha said to his servant: "Fear not: for they that be with us are more than they that be with them." This implies that along with the Syrian army came another invisible force—"they that be with them."

Who were those with them? Spiritual forces—fallen angels under Satan's command.

So although the visible threat was the Syrian army, the true threat was spiritual. Darkness had determined to silence the Word of the Lord in the mouth of the prophet. Faced with this, the Kingdom of Heaven deployed a force, because this was not merely a human battle; it required a heavenly army capable of confronting the enemy's power.

When fighting against men, a single angel is enough to destroy one hundred and eighty-five thousand (2 Kings 19:35). But when engaging in warfare in heavenly places, the demands are different—one angel is not enough for such confrontations.

That is why the mountain was full of horses and chariots of fire. They were not there for show, nor because Heaven enjoys intimidation. Their presence was necessary to defend the prophet's life, because the enemy's deployment was not small.

Therefore, there are specific battles that require the believer to request from the Kingdom of Heaven a greater force. And prayer plays a vital role in this.

The Lord Jesus said: "I could pray to my Father." The means by which we request from our Heavenly Father is prayer. It is through prayer that we ask for everything we need—including daily protection.

When the Lord taught us how to pray, He said: "And lead us not into temptation, but deliver us from evil" (Matthew 6:13). This shows that our prayers should always include a plea for deliverance from the power of the evil one.

That's why spiritual warfare must be approached with seriousness and maturity. We cannot assume that just because we are Christians, we can enter into any battle. There are conflicts for which the Kingdom of God has not authorized a deployment of force. If we foolishly enter such battles, we risk not only physical harm but also putting at risk the angel that defends us.

It is important to note that these heavenly armies are not always present with us; otherwise, the Lord would not have said that He could ask for these legions. If He said He could ask, it means they were not with Him at that moment—although He certainly had the right to summon them.

The intention of the Kingdom of God is not to appear glorious—it already is glorious, and there is no other kingdom in the universe with such majesty. Heavenly armies do not descend for display or spectacle. These kinds of armies descend in specific moments of need and are requested and administered by the authorities of the Kingdom—that is, by sons and daughters of God who have reached spiritual maturity and who understand both warfare and divine law during times of conflict.

Just as angels descended to minister to our Lord Jesus, there are also angels who minister to and defend the heirs of the Kingdom in their daily battles. However, there will be moments—specific battles—in which the need arises to request legions from Heaven. I must emphasize that this is for Christians who have reached maturity and have learned how to properly administer various conflicts.

When a Christian persists in living in a state of immaturity, without seeking growth in the knowledge of divine law, they deprive themselves of the experiences and victories that these battles could bring. Such believers are not an immediate threat to the kingdom of darkness, so there is no need for demonic troops to be deployed against them—and consequently, the Kingdom of Heaven will not need to provide such defense on their behalf either.

We see this principle in the life of Jacob. The patriarch was in imminent danger, for his brother, accompanied by four hundred men, did not come with peaceful intentions. In light of this threat, warrior angels came to Jacob's camp: "And Jacob went on his way, and the angels of God met him" (Genesis 32:1). The phrase "the angels of God met him" implies that these angels were not already with him, but were sent due to a specific danger. This does not mean Jacob was without angelic presence—without a doubt, "the angel of the Lord encampeth round about them that fear him"—but when it comes to war against the hosts of wickedness, a single angel is not enough. A full deployment of troops is required, depending on the strength of the enemy.

We cannot expose a single angel to superior forces of darkness. If we do, the angel assigned to protect us will be unable to defend effectively.

To clarify this even more, let us look at the case of Daniel in Babylon.

After searching the Scriptures, Daniel came to understand that the law granted freedom to his people. This revelation triggered a spiritual conflict through prayer: "In the third year of Cyrus king of Persia a thing was revealed unto Daniel, whose name was called

Belteshazzar; and the thing was true, but the time appointed was long: and he understood the thing, and had understanding of the vision" (Daniel 10:1). Immediately, the angel Gabriel was sent to Daniel (v. 12), but the prince of Persia opposed him for twenty-one days.

Let me explain this more clearly by quoting a modern translation that renders the verse as follows: "But the prince of the kingdom of Persia withstood me one and twenty days: but, lo, Michael, one of the chief princes, came to help me; and I remained there with the kings of Persia" (Daniel 10:13).

This reveals something significant: the kingdom of Persia was under the dominion of a fallen angel—one of very high rank and authority, for he is called a prince, meaning "first in rank."

It is essential to understand that the angels who rebelled have not lost their power. Power is something inherent to life. In the nature with which they were created, they were endowed with power—and their rebellion did not nullify their natural capabilities.

The war that the Kingdom of Heaven wages against them is based on stripping them of authority. God's judgment does not remove their power but deprives them of authority and condemns them to eternal fire.

In Daniel's case, the prince of Persia had greater strength than the angel Gabriel. The ranking power of the prince who guarded the nation of Persia surpassed the combat capacity of Gabriel, to the point that Gabriel was withheld among the kings of Persia.

In other words, he was prevented from fulfilling his mission. However, as we stated earlier, the administration of this warfare takes place on earth through the authorities of the Kingdom. "The time appointed was long" (Daniel 10:1), and Daniel's persistence in executing the legislative power—which declared the freedom of his people—could not be resisted by the powers of darkness. As a result, the Kingdom of God deployed a greater force: another prince, for it takes a prince to overcome a prince.

Let us remember: these princes do not fight alone. "And there was war in heaven: Michael and his angels fought against the dragon" (Revelation 12:7). They command forces under their authority.

Daniel's cry, fully grounded in a legal truth, gave him the authority to call for a heavenly army—an army led by the prince Michael, who cleared the way through the hostile forces for Gabriel to fulfill his mission.

In summary, we have been given authority from God to unleash spiritual conflict in heavenly realms.

However, this authority is based on knowledge of the legislative power—that is, the Word of God.

If a Christian is negligent in their pursuit of growth in the knowledge and illumination of the Word, they are disqualified from using this authority—for "the angels... do his commandments, hearkening unto the voice of his word" (Psalm 103:20).

In other words, if the president of a country issues unconstitutional orders, the military or police are not obligated to obey—because such an order violates a higher authority: the constitution.

The same principle applies in the Kingdom of Heaven: the highest authority is the Word of God. No one is above it, and the entire universe is under its dominion.

It is this very Word that has granted the believer the authority to be seated in heavenly places in Christ.

Therefore, it is unconstitutional for a Christian to issue a command, or even to make a plea or petition to the Kingdom of Heaven, without being grounded in the Scriptures.

This is why many prayers go unanswered—because they are unconstitutional.

No angel will move on your behalf if your command lacks a foundation in the Word of God, even if you are an authority in the Kingdom.

For this reason, as an authority, the Christian is called to know divine law—otherwise, we act irresponsibly.

Daniel was able to unleash a heavenly battle only after searching the writings of the prophet Jeremiah, where it was revealed that the captivity would last seventy years. This knowledge gave him the legal grounds to present a petition to Heaven—and in response to such petitions, Heaven does not hesitate to deploy whatever force is necessary to bring it to pass.

What is your battle? Examine the Scriptures carefully and build your petition to Heaven on the clear foundation of what is written.

Persevere in prayer; if there is a delay, it is because a battle is taking place in the heavens.

Without a doubt, the angel is already on his way. Persist, lest the angel be delayed in the heavenly realms.

Persist; if a greater force is needed, Heaven will send it—if your prayer is grounded in the legislative power, that is, the Word of God.

In the face of immediate danger, do not hesitate to give an executive order in the name of the Lord Jesus Christ, who is our Commander-in-Chief—for all angels are subject to Him:

"Who is gone into heaven, and is on the right hand of God; angels and authorities and powers being made subject unto him" (1 Peter 3:22).

And He has given us angels to guard us in all our ways, so that our feet do not stumble:

"They shall bear thee up in their hands, lest thou dash thy foot against a stone" (Psalm 91:12).

Chapter 2

Diseases

The establishment of the Kingdom of Heaven must be marked by two fundamental events: first, the sick are healed; and second, demons are cast out (Matthew 8:16; Matthew 10:8; Mark 1:34; Mark 6:13; Luke 10:9; Acts 5:16; Acts 19:12).

Whenever the Kingdom of God is being established in a place, it becomes evident through these two signs. We cannot boldly proclaim that the Kingdom of Heaven is among us if sickness reigns in the midst of the people. The attributes of Christ are light and life; and this light cannot be tolerated by darkness, for the light shineth in darkness; and the darkness comprehended it not (John 1:5).

Therefore, demons are compelled to flee when the light of Christ enters a place. But Christ is not only the light; He is also the life. For this reason, the sick are healed in the presence of the Lord Jesus, for sickness—being the forerunner of death—cannot stand before Him.

However, this experience seems to be fading more and more within modern-day Christianity, to the point where many no longer even seek healing through Christ, but have grown accustomed to coexisting with disease. This resignation may appear acceptable to some, but it is not acceptable for the preaching of the Kingdom of Heaven, for sickness is an affront to the life that we proclaim through our message.

In our Christian journey, we will inevitably encounter sickness in one way or another. This is part of the believer's struggle. But the key point of this chapter is how we are to confront sickness. Let us begin with the foundational truth of the Christian's right to healing. As stated in the first chapter, every manifestation of power that the Kingdom of Heaven brings to earth must be fully grounded in law—that is, in the Word of God.

The legal right that grants healing to the believer is found in the wounds of Christ. He not only suffered death but was also wounded—He was wounded for our transgressions—and bruised—He was bruised for our iniquities. He could have stopped there and simply died. Yet it was still necessary for sores to be inflicted upon His body, in order to judge sickness in His flesh. This specific kind of wound—referred to as a "stripe" or "wound"— stripped disease of its power to continue ruling in the bodies of those who accept the sacrifice of the cross (Isaiah 53:5; 1 Peter 2:24).

Nevertheless, this experience is becoming increasingly distant in the lives of many of God's children. This is mainly due to the absence of the word of revelation.

In the Word of God, there are laws that are connected to the fulfillment of additional laws. When one legal requirement for healing is met but another is completely overlooked, the healing cannot be fully effective.

For example, if a law is established somewhere stating, "Food shall be given to women over sixty years of age," there are clearly two conditions: first, to be a woman; and second, to be over sixty. If the first condition is met but not the second, the benefit is not granted.

In the same way, the Kingdom of Heaven operates through laws that function together to grant benefits to humanity. Therefore, it is essential to observe closely what the Word of God is teaching us.

In Psalm 24, a blessing is extended to man: "Who shall ascend into the hill of the Lord? or who shall stand in his holy place?" To access this benefit, the Word requires at least four legal conditions: to have clean hands, a pure heart, to not lift up the soul unto vanity, and to not swear deceitfully.

Similarly, healing also comes with joint legal requirements. If only one of these is fulfilled, we fall short of obtaining the benefit. This is why there is no set pattern for healing in Scripture. The Lord Jesus did not heal every person in the same way; the method varied depending on the situation.

To the paralytic, He first forgave his sins (Matthew 9:2). To Peter's mother-in-law, He rebuked the fever (Luke 4:39). One leper was healed through a touch (Luke 5:13), while ten others were sent to the priest (Luke 17:14). On another occasion, He cast out the spirit of infirmity (Luke 13:12).

In some cases, the sick were healed by being anointed with oil (Mark 6:13). In the case of the blind man from Bethsaida (Mark 8:23), Jesus took him out of the village and then spit on his eyes to heal him. In Mark 7:34, we read about a deaf man with a speech impediment; to heal him, Jesus looked up to heaven, sighed, and said, "Ephphatha" (be opened).

We see many different methods used by the Lord—and even by the apostles—to heal the sick.

The question we must ask is: Why these specific actions? I do not believe Jesus took the blind man out of the village and spat on his eyes just for aesthetic reasons; nor did He sigh and say "be opened" merely to impress the onlookers. Undoubtedly, that was not the case.

Each act the Lord Jesus performed to bring healing carried divine revelation. Every healing had a distinct legal requirement. Not all could be healed in the same way; and for each act, there was a meaningful reason it had to be done that way.

For instance, in the case of the paralytic, it was necessary to forgive him first, because the illness was closely connected to his sin; without forgiveness, healing would have been impossible. Or in the case of the bent-over woman, it was necessary to cast out the unclean spirit that caused the infirmity.

The issue today lies in our attempts to heal according to our own reasoning, disregarding spiritual laws. The case of the deaf and mute man clearly illustrates this modern problem:

"And they bring unto him one that was deaf, and had an impediment in his speech; and they beseech him to put his hand upon him" (Mark 7:32).

The Bible says they brought a deaf man with a speech impediment and begged Jesus to lay His hands on him.

Let us observe how human reasoning operates. The intention of these men was for Jesus to lay hands on him; but that is not what the Lord did. In fact, what He did was quite unique: He put His fingers into the man's ears, spat, and touched his tongue. Then He looked up to heaven, sighed, and said, "Ephphatha"—be opened. This was nothing like what they had expected, for they assumed it would be enough for Jesus simply to lay hands on him.

One of the main discrepancies people have today concerning the Spirit is this: they desire a formula or method to heal all the sick. And while it is true that the laying on of hands ministers healing, it is crucial to first understand the reasons behind the illness. This is why we are in desperate need of the Spirit of wisdom and revelation (Ephesians 1:17). It is the Spirit of wisdom and revelation who leads the believer in the particularities of each case, showing how to proceed. For this Spirit is the very same Christ who healed the sick two thousand years ago—and who still heals them today.

Therefore, if we lack the presence of the Spirit of revelation, it will be very difficult for anyone to experience divine healing.

We already possess the legal foundation that grants us healing: the wounds of Christ. This is the primary basis upon which we can receive the gift of healing. However, this law operates in harmony with a set of other spiritual laws, and if we are unaware of them, healing will remain nothing more than a story passed down by our forefathers. Thus, the next essential step is to be filled with the Spirit of wisdom and revelation.

How can we be filled with this Spirit? In Ephesians 1:16, the apostle Paul did not cease to give thanks and to mention the believers in Ephesus in his prayers, that they might be filled with the Spirit of wisdom and revelation.

Therefore, the channel by which we attain this is prayer—and the key to effective prayer is persistence.

We cannot expect to be filled with the Spirit of wisdom and revelation while living a prayerless or careless spiritual life. If that is the case, it is likely that sickness will linger among us far longer than it should.

It is essential to establish consistency in prayer, and without ceasing, lift our voices to God so that He may fill us with the Spirit of wisdom and revelation. Only then can we be fully equipped, case by case, to bring healing to the sick—and thus, establish the Kingdom of Heaven.

Let us now consider some of the reasons why sickness remains in the life of the believer.

Understanding the reasons behind an illness is key, for it allows us to identify the additional law that must be applied in order to experience the gift of healing. Today, it is quite common to see believers giving up in their pursuit of divine healing, settling instead for the temporary relief that medicine provides. Yet this was not the design God intended for His people. Therefore, it is vital that we understand the legal foothold sickness has, in order to revoke it.

Before continuing, I would like to briefly address the matter of faith, since in the gospel it serves as the gateway to heavenly treasures. However, among believers, faith is already present—otherwise, they wouldn't be believers. And for that reason, we approach the Lord Jesus seeking healing.

The problem arises when we abandon our faith due to a lack of visible results—and that is where the battle ends. This is why one of the phrases Jesus often used when healing was, "According to your faith be it unto you." Faith must be expressed in a pursuit that is constant and unwavering. This will eventually lead to a word of revelation that unveils the reason behind the sickness—not only bringing healing to the believer but also taking them to a deeper level of revelation for future encounters with similar situations.

But it is faith that releases the word of revelation. Without this word, we are like those who fight the wind, for we do not truly know what we are battling.

Therefore, faith is an indispensable element. However, we must not turn faith into something unattainable, as many discouraged believers do. Faith is simply believing that the Lord Jesus is your healer. And I have no doubt that the vast majority of God's children believe this.

This means we are already standing at the door of healing; now we need the word of revelation, which makes healing effective. The believer is called to believe that the Lord Jesus is his healer—but it is possible that, due to ignorance of the next step after believing, he ends up frustrated. This is something Satan uses to cause people to abandon their conviction—simply because they were unaware that what was missing was the word of revelation, which brings healing to its fulfillment.

For example, Naaman the Syrian had faith (2 Kings 5:9). Otherwise, he would not have traveled from his homeland to Israel, nor would he have paid attention to the words of the young servant girl. However, this faith alone was not sufficient—he needed a word of revelation. And here again I emphasize the point, for we continue to insist on a formula to heal all diseases. But it is not so much about a method as it is about receiving a word revealed by the Spirit.

This was Naaman's case. He believed the prophet would come out, lay hands on him, and heal him. But like many today, Naaman was unaware of the necessity of a revealed word. And because of that, he left in anger.

Brothers and sisters! Since every case is different, it is essential to have the guidance of the Holy Spirit—the Spirit of wisdom and revelation.

When the word of revelation is given, we need only to follow it—and we will witness marvelous results. For Naaman the Syrian, the word was simply to dip seven times in the Jordan River. And there is divine wisdom in this. The prophet's instruction was not arbitrary; in that prophetic act, a declaration was made in the spiritual realm that granted healing to the Syrian. Every expression has its divine order and purpose. Let us not reject it, as Naaman did.

Now that we understand this, let us consider the experience of the paralytic (Matthew 9:2). In this biblical account, something triggered the word of revelation—and it was "their faith." For when Jesus saw their faith, He said to the paralytic, "Son, be of good cheer; thy sins be forgiven thee."

These four men might have thought, "We brought him here to be healed, not to have his sins forgiven." But in this case, the man's healing was directly connected to his sins—he first needed forgiveness in order to receive healing.

There are certain kinds of sins that open the door to sickness. And as long as those sins are not confessed and forgiven, healing cannot come to the believer. A child of God may fall into one of these sins—even unknowingly—and as a result, open a door to infirmity. Perhaps prayers have been made for their healing, and faith has been exercised. That is why they have sought healing from the Lord. And although the wounds of Christ give them the right to be healed, they still do not experience it.

This is where the knowledge of a joint spiritual law is needed—in this case, the cleansing of sin. Confession and an appeal to the blood of Christ become essential in order to receive the benefit of healing.

However, a believer cannot repent of a sin they are unaware of. This is why we need the Spirit of wisdom and revelation, which is obtained through constant and fervent prayer before the Lord Jesus Christ.

It is important to clarify that the Spirit of wisdom and revelation, though it is the same Holy Spirit, operates in a different sphere or dimension. For this reason, special communion is required to access that dimension. All Christians have the Spirit of Christ: "Now if any man have not the Spirit of Christ, he is none of his" (Romans 8:9). But the Spirit of wisdom and revelation— though He is the Spirit of Christ—functions specifically in the areas of discernment and divine insight. This level is reached, as we have already mentioned, through prayer— not just any prayer, but a kind that does not give up, that does not rest, that perseveres in continual supplication to be filled with this Spirit: "That the God of our Lord Jesus Christ, the Father of glory, may give unto you the spirit of wisdom and revelation in the knowledge of him" (Ephesians 1:17).

So, if the case of the paralytic mirrors the case of a believer today, it is necessary to discern the type of sin—whether known or unknown—that has bound them to this illness. Thanks be to God, who has provided for everything, and who guarantees a complete salvation. For we have the blood of Christ, which cleanses us from all sin: "The blood of Jesus Christ his Son cleanseth us from all sin" (1 John 1:7), and "If we confess our sins, he is faithful and just to forgive us our sins, and to cleanse us from all unrighteousness" (1 John 1:9). If we confess our sins and invoke the blood of Christ, we will surely be forgiven; and once forgiven, the illness will lose its legal ground and will have to depart, in the name of Jesus.

One kind of sin that opens the door to sickness is offense between brethren: "Confess your faults one to another, and pray one for another, that ye may be healed. The effectual fervent prayer of a righteous man availeth much" (James 5:16). The healing mentioned by James involves the confession of faults. This means that resentment between brothers and sisters has the power to affect one's physical health. In order to receive healing, it is necessary to confess offenses to one another. Therefore, one must not approach prayer for the sick lightly. It is important to understand the causes of the illness. In some cases, God reveals them through conversation with the sick person; in others, He reveals them by the Spirit of revelation. If the issue involves forgiving or asking for forgiveness, healing will not manifest unless the offenses have first been confessed. This is one of the reasons why we often lack results in our prayers for healing. It is simply because joint spiritual laws are being ignored, and that may be why the answer does not come.

Another kind of sin that opens the door to sickness is murmuring against authority: "And the cloud departed from off the tabernacle; and, behold, Miriam became leprous, white as snow: and Aaron looked upon Miriam, and, behold, she was leprous" (Numbers 12:10). This is a very serious matter, for with our mouths we can bring judgment and curse upon ourselves: "Yet Michael the archangel, when contending with the devil he disputed about the body of Moses, durst not bring against him a railing accusation, but said, The Lord rebuke thee" (Jude 1:9). If we find ourselves in disagreement with those in authority over us, it is better to remain silent than to speak against them—otherwise, we risk falling under divine judgment. The principle of authority is deeply respected in the Kingdom of Heaven, for by this principle, the entire universe is kept in order.

Even Michael the archangel did not dare pronounce a curse against Satan—even though Satan is a rebellious and fallen authority. Yet because he had once held a position of authority over Michael, the archangel refrained in fear and handed over the judgment to God by saying, "The Lord rebuke thee." Despite this, many believers today do not hesitate to speak evil of their authorities—their husbands (in the case of wives), their parents (in the case of children), or their pastors (in the case of the congregation). For those who may not clearly understand what it means to curse, let me explain. The word "curse" comes from the prefix mal- and the root -speak. The prefix mal implies evil in its essence and nature, and speak refers to the act of using speech. Therefore, to curse means to speak any kind of evil over someone or something.

So when a believer speaks negatively about their parents, about their husband (in the case of married women), or about their pastor (in the context of the church), they are cursing their authority and exposing themselves to the judgment of the Kingdom of Heaven—a judgment that, in many cases, manifests as physical illness, just as it did with Miriam (Numbers 12:10).

Looking at things from this broader perspective, we begin to understand why many sick people are not healed. It is not simply a matter of praying for them or laying hands on them; we must be submitted to the joint spiritual laws that govern divine healing. In the case we just discussed, repentance and confession of such sin before the wronged authority are necessary, so that they may pray to God for the removal of the offense: "And Moses cried unto the Lord, saying, Heal her now, O God, I beseech thee" (Numbers 12:13). And after that, healing will come.

Another case of illness mentioned in the Word of God as a result of sin is partaking unworthily of the Lord's Supper: "For this cause many are weak and sickly among you, and many sleep" (1 Corinthians 11:30). One of the sins committed by the church in Corinth was the lack of reverence and discernment when partaking of the Lord's Table—to the extent that some were even getting drunk (1 Corinthians 11:21). This provoked judgment from God upon the church, to such a degree that not only were many sick, but some had even died as a result.

While I believe that such extreme cases are not as common in our time, it is still important to discern the solemnity of this sacred act. If any believer persists in treating the Lord's Supper as a common thing—without discerning the Lord's body and blood—they become guilty of the Lord's death. As in the previously mentioned cases, repentance is needed before praying for healing;

otherwise, we will not see results in our prayers and will continue praying in vain.

Envy is also counted as a sin capable of causing physical illness: "A sound heart is the life of the flesh: but envy the rottenness of the bones" (Proverbs 14:30). Many bone-related diseases may be rooted in envy, which is considered sin according to the Word of God (Romans 1:29). Therefore, a Christian who continues to harbor envy in their heart will also have to battle with sickness in their body. In such a case, it is not merely a matter of offering a prayer for healing, but rather of confessing and turning away from sin. Then, and only then, can healing be experienced.

Another reason why the believer's body may be afflicted with sickness is sorrow: "A merry heart doeth good like a medicine: but a broken spirit drieth the bones" (Proverbs 17:22). For this reason, the Lord, through the apostle Paul, commands us to rejoice: "Rejoice evermore" (1 Thessalonians 5:16). Knowing this, the enemy seeks countless ways to bring sadness into the Christian's life. And while feeling sadness is not a sin in itself, it can become sinful when the believer chooses to remain in it.

There are many reasons why sorrow may visit our lives; and although it is not wrong to feel it, we must overcome it through the joy of the Spirit.

The Lord Jesus Himself was sorrowful before His death (Mark 14:34). Yet the joy of the Spirit was present within Him to face the cross, for the Bible says: "Who for the joy that was set before him endured the cross, despising the shame" (Hebrews 12:2). Therefore, even when sorrow comes, the Christian must overcome it through joy and hope (Romans 15:13). When the believer gives in to sorrow, they abandon faith—and this becomes sin, opening the door to disease, which may consume them.

In such cases, the solution is to abandon the position of sorrow through the exercise of faith in the hope of the glory to come: "For I reckon that the sufferings of this present time are not worthy to be compared with the glory which shall be revealed in us" (Romans 8:18). When the believer is trained in this truth, they will be able to overcome sorrow and close the door to sickness.

Unconfessed sin is yet another reason why illness may attack a believer's body: "When I kept silence, my bones waxed old through my roaring all the day long" (Psalm 32:3). David testified that illness overwhelmed him while he remained silent about his sin. Likewise, disease can find a home in the body of one who refuses to acknowledge their sin—or who, knowing it, chooses to remain silent. It is very likely that such a believer will fall ill.

This is yet another reason—among many—why we may find ourselves dealing with sickness. In such cases, it is necessary to confess the hidden sin in order to receive healing. This underscores the importance of seeking out the reasons behind an illness before asking God for healing—for sickness may very well be a sign of a deeper spiritual issue.

It is also fitting to mention the matter of food, since today our physical health depends greatly on what we consume. The human body metabolizes food to extract the energy it needs to live. However, many of today's foods negatively affect our health due to chemical processes that, over time, impair the proper functioning of the body. Numerous medical professionals warn about this, yet advertising often overshadows such warnings.

To this, we must add the earth's inability to yield its fruit: "He turneth rivers into a wilderness, and the watersprings into dry ground; a fruitful land into barrenness, for the wickedness of them that dwell therein" (Psalm 107:33–34). As a result, the land requires countless chemical additives, which indirectly alter the final quality of its produce. On top of this, crops are threatened by pests, forcing farmers to spray them with harmful chemical substances, some of which are absorbed by the plants. These are the foods we consume daily to sustain ourselves.

"For every creature of God is good, and nothing to be refused, if it be received with thanksgiving: for it is sanctified by the word of God and prayer" (1 Timothy 4:4–5). Praying over our food is a serious matter. To neglect this practice is not only a lack of gratitude, but also a forfeiture of the promise given in Scripture: that food is sanctified by prayer.

We must give proper importance to this matter. Prayer over meals not only expresses our gratitude to God for His mercy and provision—it also serves the purpose of sanctifying what we eat. Sanctification means being set apart from evil. If our food must be sanctified, it is because there is some form of evil, capable of harming our bodies, attached to it. If we follow the teachings of God's Word, we can be assured that our food will be sanctified by the Word of God and by prayer.

The Lord said: "If they drink any deadly thing, it shall not hurt them" (Mark 16:18). Therefore, the Word of God and prayer have the power to cleanse our food from every harmful element.

A healthy discipline in our eating habits will help us prevent many illnesses. We must not interpret as "trials" those diseases that result from poor eating habits—such as overeating, constantly eating outside of established mealtimes, or maintaining a careless and unbalanced diet. All of these reflect a lack of responsibility in caring for our health and our bodies. We must not forget that this mortal body is the instrument through which we carry out the work of the Spirit on earth; and like any tool, if misused, it will wear out before its time.

Another case of sickness mentioned in the Bible is one caused by demons or unclean spirits: "And, behold, there was a woman which had a spirit of infirmity eighteen years, and was bowed together, and could in no wise lift up herself" (Luke 13:11). In this case, the Word of God speaks clearly of a spirit of infirmity—indicating that the matter here is entirely different from the cases previously mentioned.

Our Lord Jesus Christ knows all things, and in every case, He knew the true cause of each illness. That is why, understanding that this woman's condition was a bondage caused by a demon, He declared a word of deliverance over her. It goes without saying that there must be a very close relationship between the believer and the Lord Jesus in order to receive the revealed word concerning the case at hand—and in this way, we can be effective in Kingdom work. In these types of cases, it is not so much about praying for healing as it is about ministering deliverance. Once the person is freed from the unclean spirit, the sickness will disappear.

There are many reasons why this kind of sickness may manifest. Below are a few examples.

Some believers, in their ignorance or foolishness, have consulted with witches or spiritualists to resolve a need. Such interactions open a doorway between the believer and the unclean spirit. It is absolutely unacceptable for a Christian to consult spirits of the dead—such as "Gregorio" or others—since this is strongly condemned by Scripture: "A man also or woman that hath a familiar spirit, or that is a wizard, shall surely be put to death: they shall stone them with stones: their blood shall be upon them" (Leviticus 20:27). Under the Mosaic law, such a person was to be put to death due to the defilement caused by contact with unclean spirits.

In that time, the ministry of deliverance—as we now know it in the Church—did not yet exist. That is why death was the only possible judgment in such cases.

But this does not mean the issue is any less serious today. Although we now have the ministry of deliverance given by the Holy Spirit, the consequences of contact with an unclean spirit remain the same as they were back then.

A Christian who consults sorcerers, fortune-tellers, astrologers, or witches has given the enemy legal ground to attack them—and in some cases, these attacks will manifest as sickness, even to the point of death.

It is possible for a Christian to die before fulfilling the days appointed to them on earth, and often, this is due to spirits of death operating in their lives.

Let us remember that one of the primary purposes of the presence of the evil one in this world is to kill: "The thief cometh not, but for to steal, and to kill, and to destroy" (John 10:10). Therefore, he will seize even the smallest opportunity to take the life of a believer.

Let there be no one among us who turns to such practices as witchcraft or divination. Even consulting a horoscope to know the future is a form of divination, and it opens a doorway that leads to ruin and disease in the believer's life.

Another act that opens the door to a spirit of infirmity is rebellion, for it is closely tied to the sin of divination:

"For rebellion is as the sin of witchcraft, and stubbornness is as iniquity and idolatry. Because thou hast rejected the word of the Lord, he hath also rejected thee from being king" (1 Samuel 15:23).

This was the experience of Saul. His rebellion led him to open a door to an evil spirit that tormented him with what today might be understood as a form of schizophrenia.

Rebellion is the very foundation upon which Satan's kingdom is built; for this reason, it is placed on the same level as occultic sins.

There is no greater gateway for spirits of infirmity than rebellion.

Many Christians are consumed daily by sickness because they refuse to accept this truth—and their hearts are filled with rebellion against their pastor or spiritual leaders.

Whenever a believer gives place to rebellion, it is very common to see sickness appear in their life—or in their family.

In such cases, it is not a matter of simply praying for healing, but rather of identifying the root cause and guiding the believer through deliverance. Otherwise, the spirit of infirmity will never leave; and as a result, healing will not manifest.

It is very common today to see Christians praying for healing and never receiving it—until they give up and turn to medicine for relief, without ever obtaining an answer.

It is undeniable that healing is found in God. The issue is that, in some cases, we lack the understanding necessary to access that healing.

How good it would be to pray continually, asking God to open the eyes of our understanding, so that we might comprehend these truths!

As long as a spirit of infirmity remains in the life of a believer, that person will not be healed. Deliverance is necessary.

So, when we are faced with a case of illness, it is crucial to ask God for revelation of what is truly happening—so we may proceed accordingly.

This is acting with understanding. Otherwise, "My people are destroyed for lack of knowledge" (Hosea 4:6).

Finally, I would like to mention that there are other cases in which illnesses result from the natural wear and tear of the body—this mortal body that is destined for death:

"Now Elisha was fallen sick of his sickness whereof he died" (2 Kings 13:14).

Here we see the man upon whom a double portion of Elijah's spirit had come. Yet he was sick—and not only sick, but he died of that illness.

Therefore, we cannot say that every sickness is caused by sin or by any of the reasons previously mentioned. In Elisha's case, the illness arose simply due to the natural decay of the mortal body—a body that we all possess.

Another reason a believer may experience illness is due to a trial or divine purpose, as seen in the case of Job.

The Bible testifies that Job was a perfect and upright man before God. Yet, by God's will, Satan was allowed to afflict him with sickness.

Thus, Job's affliction was not the result of something he had done, but rather a sovereign decision from God, with an eternal purpose behind it.

We can also consider the case of Paul, who speaks of a thorn in the flesh.

Many biblical scholars agree that this thorn was likely a physical illness.

In response to this, the apostle Paul prayed three times, and on the third occasion, the purpose of the affliction was revealed to him.

From that point on, Paul chose to rejoice in his pain, his sorrow, and his affliction—so that Christ might dwell upon him more fully.

In conclusion, prayer is essential in every situation. Through prayer, God's revelation concerning the illness we are facing will come.

And once we understand the reason behind it, we will know how to respond.

In this life, we are not completely immune to sickness. However, there are illnesses that we ought not to carry.

For this reason, it is vitally important that we seek the Lord in prayer, asking for insight as to why we are sick—before we invest all our money, time, or remaining strength in the pursuit of health.

I believe it is far better to seek, through prayer, the reason for our illness. And once the Holy Spirit reveals the matter to us, we will know whether we must continue bearing that cross—or if there is something we ourselves can do to remove the root cause of the illness.

Chapter 3

Prayer: Breaking Through the Covering of the Earth

"And he will destroy in this mountain the face of the covering cast over all people, and the veil that is spread over all nations." (Isaiah 25:7)

"And he saith unto him, Verily, verily, I say unto you, Hereafter ye shall see heaven open, and the angels of God ascending and descending upon the Son of man." (John 1:51)

"And Jesus, when he was baptized, went up straightway out of the water: and, lo, the heavens were opened unto him." (Matthew 3:16)

"Oh that thou wouldest rend the heavens, that thou wouldest come down!" (Isaiah 64:1)

"And I saw heaven opened, and behold a white horse." (Revelation 19:11)

There is a necessity for the heavens to be opened in order for the Kingdom of God to operate on the earth. This is because the earth is covered, as Isaiah declares—there is a veil that envelops the world, made up of a thick darkness composed of all the operating forces of Satan in the heavenly places (Ephesians 6:12). As a result, the earth lies under deep darkness (1 John 5:19). Therefore, whenever Heaven moves to act on the earth, the heavens must be opened. This covering of darkness will be completely torn away with the establishment of Christ's Kingdom on earth (Revelation 11:15).

On the day the Lord sets Mount Zion as the highest of all mountains, the veil that covers all people will be removed. For now, every time there is a move of the Kingdom of Heaven on the earth, the heavens must be opened. Yet this opening only comes through a release of force. To make a way between Heaven and earth, there must be conflict in the air (Daniel 10:13). Whenever we speak of the heavens being opened, we are undoubtedly speaking of warfare.

One of the most powerful deaths recorded in the Bible, after that of the Lord Jesus, is the death of Stephen. His martyrdom was so violent to the kingdom of darkness that it tore the heavens open (Acts 7:56). This resulted in a great blessing for the Church in those days. Whenever the heavens are opened, it brings blessing to God's people on earth. This is why we so desperately need to see it happen more often. As God's people, we have the ability to open a way between Heaven and earth.

If we, as the Church, walked with the heavens open at all times, we would witness extraordinary things every day. The opening of Heaven is nothing more than a guarded pathway opened through the heavenly realm to allow the angels of God to bring heavenly blessings to His people. But for this path to be opened, there must be legal ground granted by man to the Kingdom of Heaven. Let me give an example to explain this more clearly.

I live in a rented house. The house is not mine—I simply pay to live in it. However, that payment gives me certain rights and privacy. If the owner of the house comes, he cannot enter the home without my permission, even though the house belongs to him. There are laws and agreements that prevent him from using his own property while it is under my jurisdiction as a tenant. If he wants to use the house, he must first ask me to vacate it.

Something similar happens in relation to the earth. It is indisputable that "The earth is the Lord's, and the fulness thereof" (Psalm 24:1). However, "The heaven, even the heavens, are the Lord's: but the earth hath he given to the children of men" (Psalm 115:16). This means that we are tenants of the earth; and so, the Kingdom of Heaven requires jurisdiction in order to act freely upon it. The other option would be to evict man from the earth—but that is not God's intention for humanity.

The problem is that Satan stole from man what rightfully belonged to him, and now "the whole world lieth in wickedness" (1 John 5:19). For this reason, he guards the earth with a covering of darkness, and his main objective is to prevent any communion between

Heaven and earth. However, the work of Christ restores the earth to the sons of men, granting them the legal right to possess it once more.

Thus, the jurisdiction needed by the Kingdom of Heaven to intervene on earth lies within mankind. This is where prayer plays a vital role.

The covering of darkness remains upon the earth in the heavenly realms. This is because many continue to live in submission to Satan. However, there is a remnant on the earth who have accepted the sacrifice of the Lord Jesus Christ, and they are claiming the earth as their inheritance—a right that heavenly law has granted them through Christ Jesus. Whenever these individuals raise a petition to Heaven, they do so on legal terms, granting Heaven the jurisdiction to act on earth on their behalf. These petitions rise through prayer—and it is constant, unwavering prayer that opens the heavens.

Though the opening is achieved by angels through warfare, it is administered by the believer through prayer. Without prayer, the Kingdom of Heaven would not have the legal jurisdiction to directly intervene for the good of mankind. It's not that prayer empowers Heaven—Heaven already possesses power sufficient to overcome every force of the enemy. The issue is not about who is stronger, but rather who has the right to act on the earth. This is a legal battle, governed by the laws of Heaven. And in the outcome of our conflicts, prayer plays an essential role.

It is prayer that grants legal right to the heavenly forces to be deployed for our help and blessing. Every time we pray in the name of the Lord Jesus Christ, we are exercising the right that Heaven has given us to claim the earth as our inheritance—provoking a response from the angels in accordance with God's law, to intervene on our behalf.

When a Christian sets their heart to pray fervently and with unshakable perseverance, the forces of darkness in the heavenly places will not be able to withstand the assault of the angels. Thus, for evil spirits, victory above becomes impossible. This leads them to redirect their attack downward—that is, toward the person who is waging war through prayer. If they manage to discourage the believer into abandoning their prayers, they will have won; or if they succeed in involving the believer in some form of sin, the prayer will lose its power and effectiveness. For this reason, one must be especially watchful when engaging in spiritual warfare through prayer. Even the slightest negligence could disqualify us from leading an effective prayer.

The primary channel through which the heavens are opened is prayer.

However, there are certain requirements for the Christian who sets themselves apart to pray, so that their prayer may be truly effective in opening the heavens. Prayer alone is not enough; there are conditions that must be met by the one who seeks to break through the heavens. Without meeting these conditions, long hours of prayer may produce little fruit. And we have seen this time and time again—believers who pray fervently, yet see few results.

It is important to consider everything that the Word of God requires of us in order to be truly effective in prayer. When a Christian succeeds in opening the heavens, many things in life begin to change. Our Lord Jesus Christ was only able to begin His public ministry the day the heavens were opened over Him (Matthew 3:16). The fullness of our ministry, the salvation of many souls, and the manifestation of the Kingdom of God in our lives can only happen if the heavens above us are opened.

1 Peter 3:7 shows us one cause that can diminish the effectiveness of a believer's prayer: conflict between spouses. It is impossible to offer an effective prayer to Heaven when strife reigns between husband and wife. It is vital to understand this clearly and to remain alert in discerning such moments when they arise. Marital

disagreements can erupt unexpectedly, often triggered by trivial matters.

So, when prayer becomes intense—so intense that it weakens the forces of the enemy—those forces will cunningly launch a counterattack against the believer in an attempt to disconnect them from their prayer life. One such tactic is to create conflict between spouses. If this is not discerned, the answer to prayer may die right there. If the wife lacks spiritual maturity—or the husband, likewise—it will be easy for the enemy to ignite conflict: a single offensive word, a bad attitude, financial stress, an unexpected visitor... any of these could be used by Satan to create an atmosphere of tension between a husband and wife.

Being watchful in these matters is crucial if we desire results in prayer. Wisdom and discernment play a critical role in such situations. Knowing how to respond to a word that comes straight from the pit of hell can make all the difference. Let us remember the case of Job: his wife was used by Satan himself to try to make him abandon his integrity. If we do not learn to discern the origin of words, we will not experience breakthrough through prayer.

Another strategy the enemy uses—when he can no longer sustain his resistance in the heavenly places—is to stir up division between brothers and sisters in the faith

(Matthew 5:23). I insist: when we are engaged in spiritual conflict through prayer, we must be watchful of what begins to arise around us. Satan is ruthless in warfare; he will use whatever is at his disposal to hold his ground.

Today, it is sadly common to find resentment among believers. I fear that this is a major reason why so many prayers are ineffective. Since this is a weapon the enemy has at his disposal to weaken our prayers, he will use it at any moment, without hesitation. When a Christian chooses to pray fervently, it is likely that gossip, slander, murmuring, or accusations will begin to arise against them. If this is not discerned, the believer's heart may become wounded and bitter—and if that happens, the enemy will have won the battle.

I understand that it is not easy to remain standing under such attacks. But if we train ourselves to discern the nature of this warfare, we will begin to see the enemy behind the hurtful words, rather than our brother or sister (1 Peter 2:23). Let us follow the example of our Lord Jesus, who was attacked in every imaginable way, yet never lost the purity of His heart. If we can continue in prayer without allowing resentment to take root, we will see great results—for it is in this way that a portal is opened in the heavenly realms. That opening becomes a channel through the thick darkness covering this world, through which angels may descend with the blessings God has prepared for us.

This principle of warfare also includes the matter of unforgiveness (Mark 11:25). A Christian who persists in holding offense against a brother or sister is a Christian who is out of the fight. They are incapable of being effective in prayer. If you have held resentment toward a family member, a neighbor, or a fellow believer, I urge you to abandon that posture and repent before the Lord. In exchange, you will reap great results through prayer.

James 5:16 says: "The effectual fervent prayer of a righteous man availeth much." Effectual prayer demands a particular quality from the one who prays: righteousness. Effectual prayer is inseparably linked to the righteous. There is no way to separate these two qualities—there can be no effective prayer without righteousness.

Knowing this, we must carefully observe our conduct, because we may be walking on the edge of injustice without even realizing it. Righteousness is giving each person what is rightly theirs. It is important to be just in our dealings—not opportunistic. Some believers take advantage of their brethren's lack by buying their belongings for far less than they are worth. This type of behavior weakens the effectiveness of prayer.

The power of prayer is directly tied to justice. As a Christian loses righteousness, so too will they lose power in their prayers. We must be careful in every area of life to ensure that righteousness is present.

For those of us who are parents, we must remember this when disciplining our children—listening carefully to each side so we do not favor one unjustly. This too is a form of injustice. We would do well to be vigilant in these matters, because injustice can slip into our lives in subtle ways, often without our noticing. This may be one of the enemy's best strategies to undermine the effectiveness of our prayers. We must keep these things in mind when we pray. Be watchful with any business deals that come our way. Otherwise, we could fall into a trap of the devil. Let's not buy something just because it's cheap—let's take the time to investigate its origin.

Many Christians, without knowing it, have purchased stolen goods simply because they were offered at a low price. In doing so, the believer becomes a participant in an act of injustice, even if unaware—and this could very well be the reason why their prayers are being withheld in the heavens.

Brothers and sisters, in spiritual warfare we must be extremely vigilant. Our adversary uses cunning to hold his position. Let us always ask God for wisdom to judge every matter with righteousness, so that our prayers may be effective.

Finally, I want to emphasize the necessity of perseverance—something the apostle Paul often urged us to practice (Colossians 4:2; Romans 12:12).

The Bible also tells us the parable of a widow who pleaded for justice against her adversary (Luke 18:3). What draws my attention in this story are the Lord's words: the need to always pray and not faint. The Lord does not command us to pray continually out of whim. If God says we must always pray and not lose heart, it is because there is a real need to do so.

And this is where many Christians lose the battle. Perhaps they lack none of the qualities mentioned earlier, but their faith is stolen because they do not know how to persist in prayer. Why, then, is there a need for persistent prayer? It is because of the spiritual conflict we have already discussed.

As parents, when we hear our child cry out, we respond immediately—we rush to their room to see what they need. And if we, being evil, do this, how much more shall your Father which is in heaven give good things to them that ask him? (Matthew 7:11).

When the children of God cry out in righteousness, our Father responds immediately (Daniel

10:12). God does not delay in answering those who do His will.

Why, then, must we insist in prayer? It is due to the presence of countless forces of darkness, which claim legal rights over the heavenly realms to obstruct the free movement of God's angels on earth. However, when prayer is offered in righteousness and holiness— persistently and on the basis of the laws that govern the Kingdom of Heaven—no evil power can withstand the force of the chief princes of God's Kingdom.

This opens a channel between Heaven and earth, allowing the light and glory of God to descend upon the believer.

In Daniel's case, the angel Gabriel said: "From the first day that thou didst set thine heart to understand, and to chasten thyself before thy God, thy words were heard, and I am come for thy words."

We see here that God's answer came at the very moment Daniel humbled himself—not a minute later. The delay was not on God's end, but in the heavenly realms (Daniel 10:13). This is the reason we are told to pray always and not to faint.

The immature or spiritually infantile Christian does not understand this and ends up blaming the Heavenly Father for not responding immediately. But in reality, if the prayer meets the requirements of the

Kingdom of Heaven, it will be answered at once. Yet, opposition exists in the spiritual realm (Ephesians 6:12).

It is perseverance in prayer that grants the believer the legal right to receive a deployment of heavenly power—power strong enough to break through the heavens and send down the provision that is needed. If Daniel had not remained in a posture of humility for twenty-one days, perhaps the release of power from the archangel Michael would not have taken place.

One of the chief enemies of effective prayer today is inconsistency. A believer who is inconsistent will lose their battles in the heavens long before the fight ever reaches the ground.

Walking under open heavens should be the daily pursuit of every Christian—something we seek with desperate longing. If through our prayers we can move the heavenly forces to open the heavens, many things in our lives will be transformed: the salvation of our families, the preaching of the gospel, our worship and praise unto the Lord—even our church gatherings will be filled with the Spirit of Life, who will convict men of sin, of righteousness, and of judgment.

Chapter 4

The Tithe as a Spiritual Principle

In this chapter, we will address the subject of the tithe as a spiritual principle rather than as a doctrine—since doctrines may differ according to dispensations, while principles remain unchanging. For example, baptism is a foundational doctrine in the dispensation of grace; however, it was never mandated under the Law, for obvious reasons. In the same way, the tithe—as a doctrine—has undergone changes depending on the priesthood. For instance, the way Abraham gave his tithe was not the same as the way the children of Israel did. Abraham tithed to the priesthood of Melchizedek, while the Israelites tithed under the Levitical priesthood.

Therefore, doctrines may vary based on the dispensation, while spiritual principles remain eternal. And it is from this perspective that we will study the subject of the tithe. For more than being a doctrine, it is a spiritual principle—and it was not only practiced by Abraham and Jacob, but existed even before them, and will continue to operate for eternity.

The practice of tithing on earth began with the formation of nations. Kings offered protection to their people, and the people were obligated to give ten percent of their labor as tribute (1 Samuel 8:15).

Governments were established to provide protection, and this has remained the case from the beginning of nations to this day—the only difference being that the percentage of taxation varies depending on the nation.

The key point is that every citizen is required to contribute to their nation. In turn, the nation is responsible for providing protection and welfare within its territory.

It would be unjust for a citizen to steal from the State, since every citizen benefits from its protection. For example: if I arrive home and discover that a thief has broken in, my immediate reaction will be to call the police. Most likely, within minutes, agents of the State will arrive.

However, they will not ask whether I have paid my taxes faithfully. No—they will simply do their job. Nevertheless, every police officer receives a salary from the State. Where does that money come from? It comes from the taxes paid by citizens.

Therefore, it is unjust to make use of the State's protection while refusing to contribute to it.

There are many other services the State is obligated to provide to its citizens, such as infrastructure, housing, healthcare, education, security, and more.

In our country, much of the healthcare system is subsidized by the government. Every time a citizen visits a doctor, that consultation—or the medicine they receive—is paid for by the State.

Thus, it is not right for someone to enjoy, whether in great or small measure, the benefits provided by the State while avoiding their civic responsibility to pay taxes.

Whenever we use transportation, we realize that we travel on paved roads, over bridges and through tunnels—necessary infrastructure for mobility, both within and outside the cities.

The use of all these benefits is made possible through the contributions of each citizen. Again, I stress: it is unjust to take advantage of these things while evading taxes.

As citizens, we have a need for these services, but we also have an obligation to contribute.

This is not a favor we do for the State, but a duty we have as citizens.

For this reason, tax evasion is considered a crime that may even be punished with imprisonment.

Let us now consider this from a biblical perspective. As Christians, we hold dual citizenship (Philippians 3:20).

In natural terms, we belong to a nation of this world; in my case, I am Colombian.

However, upon receiving Christ, we obtain a second citizenship—we are placed under a government called the Kingdom of Heaven.

This is not an abstract or mystical government; it is, simply put, a government—and one that holds far greater weight than any other in the universe.

Thus, the tax system of this Kingdom does not pertain only to one territory on earth, but encompasses the entire universe.

Even the children of the mighty are obligated to give unto the Kingdom of Heaven: "Give unto the Lord, O ye mighty, give unto the Lord glory and strength" (Psalm 29:1).

Some Christians interpret being under grace as meaning the end of tithing.

However, the tithe is something intrinsically tied to the Kingdom. Whenever we speak of the tithe, we are speaking of the Kingdom.

The Kingdom and grace are distinct matters; we must not confuse the function of grace with the operation of the Kingdom.

We must not think that being under grace means we are no longer under the Kingdom.

Let us pause to reflect on this before moving forward, so that we may better understand what follows.

The Kingdom of God is from eternity to eternity, while grace is a gift granted to man because of his inability; nevertheless, grace does not negate the Kingdom—in fact, the Kingdom is above grace.

Grace came for the sake of the Kingdom, not the Kingdom for the sake of grace.

Humanity was created and placed under the order of the Kingdom, to exercise authority over the earth.

However, man's fall disqualified him from remaining in the Kingdom. Therefore, God's plan to restore man to the Kingdom was to bring grace.

What, then, is grace?

In broad terms, grace is God's action in Christ Jesus to forgive and atone for iniquity—bringing man to judgment in the death of Christ, and imparting to him a new nature through the Holy Spirit, one which enables him to obey all the requirements of the Kingdom.

Thus, the goal is always the Kingdom.

Grace is God's channel to restore man's position within the Kingdom.

Without grace, man would have no access to the Kingdom.

So grace does not annul the Kingdom; rather, it affirms it.

Being under grace does not mean being free from the demands of the Kingdom—it means being empowered by the Holy Spirit for full obedience to it.

As we have already mentioned, the tithe is intimately connected to the Kingdom. We cannot speak of the Kingdom of God without speaking of the tithe. This is why Abraham tithed to Melchizedek, who appeared not only as a priest but also as a king (Genesis 14:18). When we speak of the tithe, we speak of the Kingdom; and when we speak of the Kingdom, we speak of protection and provision, among other things. This is why Jacob's vow involved receiving protection and provision in exchange for tithing. In other words, Jacob was wandering without a kingdom to protect him—so when he had a vision of the Kingdom of God, he offered to come under that Kingdom. How? Through tithing. If the Kingdom of God accepted Jacob's tithe, it would be obligated to protect and provide for him. There is great revelation in this.

The practice of tithing was also given to the nation of Israel, to legally establish them under the Kingdom of God. This brought with it the guarantee of the protection and provision that the Kingdom is obligated to provide to its citizens. One of the reasons Israel was handed over to plunderers and thieves was because they abandoned the practice of tithing.

Let us return to the example of earthly nations. A person who evades their obligations to the State becomes a target. At any moment, their possessions can be seized, and much of their wealth may be compromised. In our country, there is a tax called VAT. Some people habitually evade it because it makes their purchases cheaper. However, when such merchandise is transported through the country, it is completely unprotected and can be confiscated at any time—because it lacks legal standing to be traded.

Something similar happens in the Kingdom of God. A Christian has been made a citizen of the Kingdom, and with that citizenship come benefits—but also responsibilities, among them the spiritual principle of giving to the Lord. When a believer tithes, they are publicly acknowledging that they are under a Kingdom that is not of this world. Their act declares that they give tribute to another Kingdom, beyond their earthly citizenship. This obligates that Kingdom to release all the benefits it owes to its citizens.

When a Christian—fully aware of this truth—persists in refusing to give tribute to the Lord, their provision and protection may be seriously affected.

These laws are well known in the heavenly realms. One reason a believer's blessing may be delayed on its way to earth is this very issue. The Bible speaks in

Malachi 3 of "the devourer." Who is the devourer? It is nothing more than a dark spiritual entity assigned to inspect which citizens of the Kingdom of God are not fulfilling their financial responsibilities, in order to confiscate their goods in the heavenly places.

Jacob understood this, which is why he said: "If God will be with me, and will keep me in this way that I go, and will give me bread to eat, and raiment to put on" (Genesis 28:20). In this case, Jacob linked his protection and provision to his tithe. He knew the principle and appealed to its benefits. Let us not give the enemy an opportunity to withhold from us what rightfully belongs to us—because the devourer will carefully examine our conduct concerning our responsibility as citizens of the Kingdom. If we are negligent in this, the enemy will find grounds to seize our blessings.

It is important to note that the tithe is not a voluntary offering, as some believe, but rather a compulsory tribute of every citizen of the Kingdom of Heaven—since they enjoy all the benefits that this citizenship provides. It is not fair to expect the angels to rush to our defense when we need protection, healing, provision, direction, and every other benefit the Kingdom of Heaven offers its citizens, if we are unwilling to acknowledge our financial responsibility.

Another key point that must be mentioned is that this must be done by faith. "Whatsoever is not of faith is sin" (Romans 14:23). The tithe is an obligation, but it must be fulfilled in faith—believing in the reality of this principle. And without a doubt, we will see extraordinary results regarding the Kingdom of God.

Finally, I want to address the tithe in the context of future dispensations. As stated earlier, the tithe as a spiritual principle remains forever. Even in the New Jerusalem, when eternity is established, the tithe will still exist (Revelation 21:24). However, some things will change with the full manifestation of the Kingdom of Heaven on earth. Christians will receive the Kingdom, and their dwelling will be with the Lord on Mount Zion.

At present, the nations of the earth do not tithe to the Lord. This practice is currently expressed only within the Church, by believers. However, when the Lord returns, Christians will no longer be the ones giving the tithe, but rather the ones receiving it from all nations (Isaiah 60:5–6; Isaiah 60:11; Isaiah 61:6):

"But ye shall be named the Priests of the Lord: men shall call you the Ministers of our God: ye shall eat the riches of the Gentiles, and in their glory shall ye boast yourselves."

If we learn this principle in this present dispensation, then when the Kingdom is fully manifested, we will be seated in places of honor—and we will completely fulfill the word that the Lord Jesus spoke to Peter: "What thinkest thou, Simon? of whom do the kings of the earth take custom or tribute? of their own children, or of strangers?" (Matthew 17:25).

But for now, it is necessary for us to "fulfill all righteousness" (Matthew 3:15). Let us be faithful to the Lord; let us submit ourselves with reverence under His Kingdom—and we shall eat the riches of the nations, and in their glory we shall be exalted.

Chapter 5
Spoils of Battle and Spoils of War

Wherever there is a battle, there are also spoils (Numbers 31:11; Luke 11:22). Many biblical texts speak to us about this reality. Whenever we talk about battle, there are unquestionably spoils that follow. The terms "battle" or "war" are quite familiar to the Christian life (1 Timothy 6:12; 2 Timothy 4:7; Ephesians 6:12). In fact, they are at the very heart of the believer's journey.

A war is made up of many battles; and there is a difference between the spoils of a battle and the spoils of a war.

The spoils of war are always greater, because they include the full treasure of the enemy—while the spoils of a single battle consist only of what the enemy's troops brought with them to the field.

Put another way: a battle is a confrontation between two adversaries. Whoever wins takes the spoils of that particular battle, meaning whatever possessions the enemy had with them at the time.

War, on the other hand, is the complete defeat and destruction of the adversary. The spoils of war are far greater, including not only the opponent's possessions on the battlefield, but also all that belonged to him: his territories, his wealth, his cities—absolutely everything that was under his ownership now becomes the inheritance of the victor.

Therefore, the spoils of war are greater than the spoils of a single battle.

However, to win the war, one must first win many battles. In this chapter, we will consider what our spoils are when we win a battle—and when we win the war.

Our struggle is not against flesh and blood (Ephesians 6:12), but against forces of darkness. These forces are structured in ranks of authority, and behind them is a vast multitude of wicked spiritual hosts. These are our true enemies.

Throughout the history of humanity, there has been war between mankind and Satan. Many of these battles have been won by the powers of darkness. This means the spoils of those battles have been claimed by the enemy.

The first battle between man and Satan took place in the Garden of Eden. Unfortunately for us, Adam was defeated, and the spoils of the battle fell into Satan's hands.

It was a massive spoil. Had man won this battle, he would have been positioned above all principalities and powers—including Satan himself. That was the spoil at stake.

But since Adam was defeated, it was Satan who claimed the spoils of that battle. These included his life and that of his descendants, his peace, and one of the most precious possessions—not only for man but also for God: the earth. All of this came under Satan's dominion.

This is how "the whole world lieth in wickedness" (1 John 5:19).

Thanks be to God for the last Adam, Christ Jesus, who confronted the enemy once again and recovered not only what was lost, but also claimed the spoils of the battle—being seated "far above all principality, and power" (Ephesians 1:21).

Just as Adam and Christ fought this battle, we as Christians must fight many battles before winning the war.

Each battle has its spoils—whether for us or for the enemy. It is important to note that these battles are closely related to descendants, due to the unity that characterizes the human race.

The way man was created makes him part of a collective unity. This is due to his capacity to reproduce— thereby extending his own life.

That is why, when Satan defeated Adam in the garden, we were all defeated with him.

The Bible also tells us that Levi paid tithes when Abraham gave tithes to Melchizedek, even though Levi had not yet been born; nevertheless, he was in Abraham (Hebrews 7:9).

In the same way, though we were not yet born, we were in Adam when he was defeated. This is the divine design by which the human race was created. This unity creates a gap that the enemy can exploit in order to claim future generations as his spoils.

Let us remember that it is in the moment of testing that the enemy takes the opportunity to tempt us:

"Blessed is the man that endureth temptation: for when he is tried, he shall receive the crown of life, which the Lord hath promised to them that love him" (James 1:12).

Later in the same chapter, James tells us that God tempts no one. However, Scripture does affirm that God tests us.

Why, then, are both testing and temptation mentioned together in this passage?

This is because the enemy waits for moments of divine testing in order to launch his temptation—seeking to defeat us and steal what God has given us.

To illustrate this, let us consider an example:

Suppose a man, as the head of his household, is being tested in the area of his finances, resulting in a period of temporary lack. The enemy will present various proposals—one of which may be to gain money through illegitimate means.

If the father yields to this proposal, he will have been defeated in that battle. Satan will then have the legal right to the spoils, which in this case would be dominion over his financial system.

To perpetuate this across generations, the adversary will seek to gain certain rights—such as the ability to influence the children to fall into the same sin (iniquity).

Second, he will seek the legal right to retain what was stolen within the family line—securing his control over the family's finances.

For example, if with this illegitimately obtained money a house was purchased, the enemy's strategy will be to preserve that house as family property. This is the evidence of the father's defeat—and through it, he will control the family's financial supply, leading to long-term lack.

Adam sinned as a figure of authority. For this reason, when he fell, everything under his dominion fell with him.

Death did not touch only Adam and Eve—it extended to all creation, including the animals and the trees.

This happened because Adam was the head and authority over all earthly creation.

If you live in a house that was inherited from your parents or grandparents, it is important to investigate how that property was acquired.

If your life has been marked by persistent financial lack, this may be one of the contributing reasons—among others.

Perhaps this is why your financial condition has never improved, despite hard work, effort, and all the administrative strategies you've implemented.

If this is your case, it would be wise to consider this possibility.

Practically speaking, the next step would be to investigate how the place where you live—or any property you've inherited—was originally acquired. Bring this before God in prayer, asking Him to reveal whether there is any injustice tied to it.

We must not allow room for defeat. If the Christian wins this battle, they will gain the spoils. These include not only the restoration of financial health, but also every economic blessing stolen from their ancestors, and authority over spirits of theft and ruin—which will lose all power to attack again.

Satan knows that when he pushes a Christian into battle, there's a chance he could lose. If the believer emerges victorious, those spirits will fall completely under their authority:

"While they promise them liberty, they themselves are the servants of corruption: for of whom a man is overcome, of the same is he brought in bondage" (2 Peter 2:19).

As a result, those demons will no longer have any ability to influence that believer.

To discern whether you are under such an attack—as described in the example—it is important to observe certain patterns or symptoms, such as ongoing financial lack throughout the years. It doesn't matter where you work or live; the situation never seems to change. Another common sign is a constant pull from the enemy to borrow money, without the means to repay—thus creating a growing generational bondage.

If this is your experience, you should examine everything you've inherited from previous generations whose origin you may not know—such as a house, a car, a piece of land. Any kind of inheritance with an unknown background could be a sign of spoils seized by the enemy during a past spiritual defeat.

If, after investigating, you discover that such property or asset was acquired unjustly, it is important—when possible—to make restitution. This is part of the battle. Restitution means repaying the true value of what was taken, along with an additional amount as compensation:

"Then they shall confess their sin which they have done: and he shall recompense his trespass with the principal thereof, and add unto it the fifth part thereof, and give it unto him against whom he hath trespassed" (Numbers 5:7).

"And if he that sanctified the house will redeem his house, then he shall add the fifth part of the money of thy estimation unto it, and it shall be his" (Leviticus 27:15).

"And Zacchaeus stood, and said unto the Lord; Behold, Lord, the half of my goods I give to the poor; and if I have taken any thing from any man by false accusation, I restore him fourfold" (Luke 19:8).

It is necessary to seek out the person who was defrauded. If that person has died, one must approach an heir. And if there is absolutely no way to find anyone from that family, the money should be brought as an offering to the Lord, including the restitution amount, and presented before a church authority, so that they may remit the offense to the cross of Calvary (John 20:23).

As this process begins, the enemy will attack—because he knows that the loss of his spoils is near. In light of this, one must have unwavering determination.

One of the weapons Satan will use is the same he used at the beginning: to besiege. It is very common to see, at this stage of the process, that the few remaining financial doors begin to close. It is important to persist in both prayer and the intention to make restitution.

If it is necessary to sell what was illegitimately acquired in order to obtain the funds, do not hesitate to do so. The sooner restitution is made, the sooner Satan's power over your finances will be shattered.

We must not fear the loss of any material possession on this earth. If it becomes necessary to sell what we own in order to make restitution, we must be willing to do it.

After making restitution, it is important to reflect on how far this influence has shaped our financial behavior—bringing to mind any debts or financial commitments we've failed to fulfill due to the same pattern of lack.

In response, one must spend quality time in prayer. The enemy, in his desperation, will attempt to dry up every source of provision, even to the point where one cannot buy food for the family.

However, this is nothing more than a smokescreen intended to discourage us from our purpose. If we persist in prayer, the Lord will provide all that we need in the midst of this battle.

Once the process is completed, it is necessary to make a prayer of deliverance, confessing all the wrongs—ours and those of our ancestors—declaring victory over the battle our forefathers lost, and claiming the spoils that now belong to us because we have won the battle.

Without a doubt, the demons that had held our finances for years will be forced to release them—along with everything they withheld from our ancestors. These demons will no longer have influence over our lives, for they will be entirely under our dominion (2 Peter 2:19).

Every believer must fight their own battles, and every battle has its own spoils. Today, there is one battle that the vast majority of men must face: the battle of pornography.

Now more than ever, Satan has unleashed a massive army charged with pushing God's people into the grip of pornography. When a Christian is defeated in this battle, the victorious demons claim the spoils. These consist primarily of the sexual health of the home and of the children.

One of the most common consequences experienced by a believer who has lost this battle is the loss of sexual satisfaction with their spouse. When a man falls into these snares, he opens the door to spiritual plunderers.

This also affects the believer's effectiveness in prayer, as their conscience becomes defiled and lustful desires begin to dominate them. In extreme cases, this may even lead to adultery—bringing ruin upon the children.

However, the believer who wins this battle will receive what rightfully belongs to him: his sexual health and the ability to enjoy, together with his spouse, the pleasure that marriage affords.

And something very important: he will have total dominion over every spirit of pornography and sexual disorder. This, especially in relation to the family, is indispensable in the midst of this crooked generation— particularly for the protection of the children.

A Christian who has conquered this battle has full authority to prevent any spirit of pornography or sexual disorder from approaching their children.

Because these spirits are now under his authority, they have no choice but to obey—thus creating a spiritual barrier that protects the children in the midst of a perverse generation.

Perhaps many children of believers have fallen into the traps of pornography or fornication because their parents secretly held on to sexual sins—thereby forfeiting their authority over these types of spirits.

There is no spiritual authority in a father who watches pornography to command demons not to approach his children. It is impossible.

Such a man has already opened the door to his goods by being defeated in battle. For him, there is no alternative but to be plundered.

However, if he reacts in time and engages in a worthy battle, the Holy Spirit will grant him the strength to emerge victorious.

In all of this, it is essential to develop a spiritual perspective—otherwise, we will neither understand the conflict nor recognize the enemy. Every believer is called to fight their own battles. What is your battle? It is important to develop vision in the Spirit. For some women, their battle is their husband—and their spoil is his conversion.

However, in many cases, these processes are delayed because the battle is not fought correctly, and spiritual battles become domestic arguments.

When we learn to identify the true enemy, the battle becomes much more effective. Many of the words that come from the mouth of an unbelieving spouse are actually inspired by the evil spirit battling against the believer.

But if we fail to discern this, we attack the person—allowing the enemy to win the battle and claim his spoil, which in this case is the believer's peace.

Many Christians have no peace in their homes because Satan has plundered them—even though the Lord said, "Peace I leave with you, my peace I give unto you" (John 14:27). This peace that the Lord left for the believer has, in some cases, been taken as spoil by the enemy—simply because a Christian did not know how to fight a particular battle.

Therefore, if your battle is to win your spouse for the Lord, be careful in moments of conflict or provocation—do not respond in the same manner. Rather, always use the Word of God, which is the sword of the Spirit. Harsh or cursing words usually come from darkness—but if we respond with blessing, we are gaining ground in the battle (1 Peter 3:9).

Each time we win a battle, we gain the right to spoils and authority over a particular kind of demonic nature. In this way, we grow in empowerment within the Kingdom of Heaven. There are many types of battles, too many to list—but you know what your battles are. Do not underestimate them. Give them the attention they deserve, and God will grant you the wisdom and revelation needed to overcome.

As we mentioned at the beginning of this chapter, the spoils of war are greater than the spoils of a battle. The spoils of war consist of the entirety of the enemy's possessions. It is important to win battles—but even more important to win the war. Satan's spoils are primarily composed of all the kingdoms of the world (Matthew 4:8). These kingdoms comprise 194 countries—of which 193 have come under direct influence of darkness. One of them belongs to the Lord:

"But now thus saith the Lord that created thee, O Jacob, and he that formed thee, O Israel, Fear not: for I have redeemed thee, I have called thee by thy name; thou art mine" (Isaiah 43:1).

This is Israel. However, due to its continual rebellion, God handed it over to plunderers, and it has fallen under the influence of the wicked one:

"And now go to; I will tell you what I will do to my vineyard: I will take away the hedge thereof, and it shall be eaten up; and break down the wall thereof, and it shall be trodden down" (Isaiah 5:5)—until the time of restoration.

Thus, from a physical perspective, the spoils Satan possesses are the kingdoms of this world; and from a spiritual perspective, they are the heavenly dominions that were entrusted to him. These 194 countries make up the world—and "the whole world lieth in wickedness" (1

John 5:19). Within these kingdoms lie the riches of the nations (Isaiah 60:5), and these riches are currently under the control of the enemy. He exerts influence over humanity through them.

Someone once said, "If you want to know who rules the world, follow the money." This is because of the demonic influence currently held over the wealth of the earth—since it remains under Satan's dominion.

Therefore, to take possession of the wealth, one must defeat the one who holds it:

"Or else how can one enter into a strong man's house, and spoil his goods, except he first bind the strong man? and then he will spoil his house" (Matthew 12:29).

In order to plunder the strong man, the Bible says he must first be bound. Revelation 20:3 reveals to us that Satan will indeed be bound. Once bound, he can be stripped of his spoils—composed of the kingdoms of this world and their glory (Matthew 4:8).

After this, Christ will claim the spoils for Himself—and the kingdoms of the world, along with their riches, will become the property of Christ:

"And the seventh angel sounded; and there were great voices in heaven, saying, The kingdoms of this world are become the kingdoms of our Lord, and of his Christ; and he shall reign for ever and ever" (Revelation 11:15).

The good news for us is that the spoils will be shared with the strong (Isaiah 53:12). In other words, the 194 countries on this earth—along with their wealth—will be divided by Christ among His mighty ones:

"And he that overcometh, and keepeth my works unto the end, to him will I give power over the nations" (Revelation 2:26);

"But ye shall be named the Priests of the Lord: men shall call you the Ministers of our God: ye shall eat the riches of the Gentiles, and in their glory shall ye boast yourselves" (Isaiah 61:6);

"If we suffer, we shall also reign with him: if we deny him, he also will deny us" (2 Timothy 2:12);

"And hast made us unto our God kings and priests: and we shall reign on the earth" (Revelation 5:10);

"And I saw thrones, and they sat upon them, and judgment was given unto them: and I saw the souls of them that were beheaded for the witness of Jesus, and for the word of God... and they lived and reigned with Christ a thousand years" (Revelation 20:4).

It is important to clarify that this first spoil is composed of all the kingdoms that are currently upon the earth. I mention this because, at some point in our Christian journey, many of us were taught a belief that

Scripture does not support—namely, that the Church will go to live in heaven and remain there forever with God.

However, this is not what the prophets foretold. And although it is true that "our conversation is in heaven" (Philippians 3:20), we are the ones waiting for it—not the other way around. It is we who await our heavenly citizenship.

This means that it will come to us: "And I John saw the holy city, new Jerusalem, coming down from God out of heaven, prepared as a bride adorned for her husband" (Revelation 21:2). The holy city will descend from heaven.

This is not to say that the Church will not be raptured—indeed, it will be. But only for a period of time, to be transferred to the judgment seat of Christ and determine who among the saints are the mighty ones worthy of receiving a share in the spoils:

"For we must all appear before the judgment seat of Christ; that every one may receive the things done in his body, according to that he hath done, whether it be good or bad" (2 Corinthians 5:10);

"Therefore will I divide him a portion with the great, and he shall divide the spoil with the strong; because he hath poured out his soul unto death, and he was numbered with the transgressors; and he bare the sin of many, and made intercession for the transgressors" (Isaiah 53:12).

After this, the Church will descend again to the earth:

"And the armies which were in heaven followed him upon white horses, clothed in fine linen, white and clean" (Revelation 19:14), to take possession of it—that is, the kingdoms of the world along with their riches (Revelation 5:10).

God's purpose is for us to reign with Christ upon the earth and take possession of its riches (Revelation 5:12). These riches will be free from Satan's influence and will be sanctified to be taken by the Lamb who was slain—for justice and peace among all nations:

"Of the increase of his government and peace there shall be no end, upon the throne of David, and upon his kingdom, to order it, and to establish it with judgment and with justice from henceforth even for ever. The zeal of the Lord of hosts will perform this" (Isaiah 9:7).

Thus, God's plan is not to take His Church away to heaven—but rather, to bring heaven to earth:

"And I heard a great voice out of heaven saying, Behold, the tabernacle of God is with men, and he will dwell with them, and they shall be his people, and God himself shall be with them, and be their God" (Revelation 21:3).

God has a very specific interest in the earth—a deep affection. And if we believe that we will leave this place never to return, we are, quite frankly, far from understanding the heart of the Lord.

This first war-spoil will be taken by the mighty ones from among God's people, led by Christ:

"And from the days of John the Baptist until now the kingdom of heaven suffereth violence, and the violent take it by force" (Matthew 11:12).

This kingdom on the earth will last one thousand years, before entering into the second phase of stripping Satan of the totality of his war spoils.

Once that time has been fulfilled, Satan will be released to lead one final attempt to defeat the heirs of the Kingdom—but it will only result in his complete and final defeat:

"And when the thousand years are expired, Satan shall be loosed out of his prison,

And shall go out to deceive the nations which are in the four quarters of the earth, Gog and Magog, to gather them together to battle: the number of whom is as the sand of the sea.

And they went up on the breadth of the earth, and compassed the camp of the saints about, and the beloved city: and fire came down from God out of heaven, and devoured them.

And the devil that deceived them was cast into the lake of fire and brimstone, where the beast and the false prophet are, and shall be tormented day and night for ever and ever" (Revelation 20:7–10).

This will bring about the seizure of the totality of the spoils—which includes the heavenly realms and their glory:

"Thou art the anointed cherub that covereth; and I have set thee so: thou wast upon the holy mountain of God; thou hast walked up and down in the midst of the stones of fire" (Ezekiel 28:14).

For this to be fulfilled, the physical must be removed and the spiritual established. Until that moment, the earth as we know it will continue to exist. After God's holy people have ruled on the earth for a thousand years, it will cease to exist as it currently is— because this present earth is only a shadow of the true land: incorruptible and indestructible.

Just as there was a physical tabernacle—merely a shadow of the one Moses saw on the mountain—and just as there is an earthly Mount Zion, there is also a spiritual Mount Zion that will endure forever.

This world is nothing more than a model of what truly exists:

"Who serve unto the example and shadow of heavenly things, as Moses was admonished of God when he was about to make the tabernacle: for, See, saith he, that thou make all things according to the pattern shewed to thee in the mount" (Hebrews 8:5).

When Satan makes his final attempt, it will be for his total destruction—and all that is a shadow will be removed:

"And this word, Yet once more, signifieth the removing of those things that are shaken, as of things that are made, that those things which cannot be shaken may remain" (Hebrews 12:27).

The earth will be destroyed (2 Peter 3:10–12), so that the eternal may be established—that is, a new earth where righteousness dwells (2 Peter 3:13; Isaiah 65:17; Revelation 21:1).

Upon this new earth will be established the Holy City, the New Jerusalem. The Lord will dwell in her, and from there He will rule over the entire universe together with His people.

So, if we think there are riches in this world—let us wait until we see the heavenly ones, and we will be astonished by the glory of God revealed in the heavens:

"The heavens declare the glory of God; and the firmament sheweth his handywork" (Psalm 19:1).

All of this is part of the spoils of our war. So let us ask ourselves: Is it worth fighting for? Without a doubt—it is!

"For I reckon that the sufferings of this present time are not worthy to be compared with the glory which shall be revealed in us" (Romans 8:18).

If we are valiant in the war, the Lord will grant us the victory—and we shall have a portion in this spoil.

Chapter 6
Unclean Places

"When ye be come into the land of Canaan, which I give to you for a possession, and I put the plague of leprosy in a house of the land of your possession;

And he that owneth the house shall come and tell the priest, saying, It seemeth to me there is as it were a plague in the house" (Leviticus 14:34).

We have heard much about leprosy as a disease that afflicts humans, but little has been said about a type of leprosy that manifests in houses. Here we find a deeper principle related to the spiritual atmosphere that can exist within a home.

The liturgical practices of the Law serve as didactic illustrations that convey spiritual truths. In other words, they are shadows that teach us eternal realities of a spiritual nature. In 1 Corinthians 9:9, Paul references the passage in Deuteronomy 25:4: "Thou shalt not muzzle the ox when he treadeth out the corn." He explains that this was written for the sake of those who labor in the work of God's kingdom. Thus, behind the command lies a deeper truth. The point was not so much about the welfare of oxen, but about the provision for those who serve the Lord.

The same principle is at work in the case of leprosy found in a house. It was the physical manifestation of a spiritual problem affecting that household. In some cases, it could be resolved easily; in others, the only solution was to tear the house down. This is how the people of Israel became aware of a malignant contamination within a dwelling.

Scripture consistently associates leprosy with sin; and where there is sin, demons find a place to inhabit. Therefore, a house with signs of leprosy indicated that something related to sin was defiling that space. This could be due to certain practices or the presence of abominable objects within it—such as idols, images of false gods, or other causes.

It is important to emphasize that, in some cases, the evil committed within a house could be so great that no purification was possible. The only solution was to destroy it completely and cast its remains into unclean places:

"And he shall break down the house, the stones of it, and the timber thereof, and all the mortar of the house; and he shall carry them forth out of the city into an unclean place" (Leviticus 14:45).

This principle remains just as true today as it was in ancient times. There are places that are not pleasing to the Lord, and it is essential to pay attention to this—

whether buying a new home, renting a property, or especially when choosing a place for preaching or congregating the church. To gather in a location under demonic influence may result in great spiritual setback.

Some locations have been so exposed to evil that they cannot be cleansed.

"Because of the wrath of the Lord it shall not be inhabited, but it shall be wholly desolate: every one that goeth by Babylon shall be astonished, and hiss at all her plagues" (Jeremiah 50:13).

"Ashkelon shall see it, and fear; Gaza also shall see it, and be very sorrowful, and Ekron; for her expectation shall be ashamed; and the king shall perish from Gaza, and Ashkelon shall not be inhabited" (Zechariah 9:5).

For this reason, it is vital to seek the Lord through prayer when choosing a new place to live—whether for our family or for the church. In many cases, it is indeed possible to cleanse a place:

"No foot of man shall pass through it, nor foot of beast shall pass through it, neither shall it be inhabited forty years" (Ezekiel 29:11).

"But he shall let go the living bird out of the city into the open fields, and make an atonement for the house: and it shall be clean" (Leviticus 14:53).

How does this apply today? The spiritual principles revealed in Scripture are eternal. What matters is that we understand them, even though the external practices may differ according to the dispensation of time. While the rituals may change throughout God's appointed eras, the underlying principles of liturgical instruction remain constant.

The principle revealed here is this: a house can become contaminated, and that house can contaminate its inhabitants. The definition of an unclean or defiled house is, essentially, the presence of evil spiritual entities cohabiting within it—exerting influence or promoting behavior contrary to God's design among its residents.

How can a house become defiled? Can a house truly be contaminated? Can the house of a Christian be co-inhabited by unclean spirits? We must remember that every action of the enemy against a believer must be legally justified.

In the battle against demonic spirits, sincerity is not enough. We must also vigilantly observe the principles that evil clings to in order to attack us. In other words: we may be sincere Christians, but if darkness has a legal right to be present in our home, it will surely claim it.

The conflict between the Kingdom of Heaven and the kingdom of darkness also involves a battle for geographical territory. Scripture refers to the prince of Greece and the prince of Persia—spiritual forces (Daniel

10:20). In the case of the man possessed in Gadara, the demons pleaded with the Lord, "Send us not out of the country" (Mark 5:10). And in Revelation 11:15, a powerful proclamation is made:

"The kingdoms of this world are become the kingdoms of our Lord, and of his Christ".

This shows that the spiritual conflict has direct interest in geographical points on the earth—because from there, demonic forces can exercise influence over the people. Evil does not exert the same kind of influence in America as it might in Asia, or vice versa. Certain places carry a greater propensity to drive people toward specific types of evil—because of the spiritual powers dominating those regions.

The smallest fraction of any geography is a house; it is the basic unit of a governmental system. Consequently, there is a battle to establish a spiritual atmosphere in every home on earth.

Knowing the importance of this, the kingdom of darkness works tirelessly to develop strategies that grant them legal rights to claim the spiritual environment of a household. Their tricks are countless, their inventions innumerable, and all are based on deception and lies.

How can a house become defiled? The methods are truly many, and darkness continues to develop more each day. However, we will examine the most notable in this section.

Occult practices such as the worship of idols, graven images, or any form of invocation to false gods create defilement that can cling to the physical environment of a house and remain there. Similarly, immoral acts—such as homosexuality, orgies, bestiality, incest, and sexual assault—grant demons the right to remain attached to the very walls that mark the boundaries of a dwelling.

When a cult has been particularly intense—especially in the case of satanic worship, where all forms of sexual perversion and inhuman practices are committed—the perimeter of that house becomes so spiritually contaminated that evil spirits secure legal grounds to remain in that location, even after the occupants have changed.

The extremity of such acts defiles the atmosphere, regardless of whether those practices continue. An example of this is seen in the destruction of Sodom and Gomorrah, as declared in Jeremiah 49:18:

"As in the overthrow of Sodom and Gomorrah and the neighbour cities thereof, saith the Lord, no man shall abide there, neither shall a son of man dwell in it."

In those cities, no human being ever lived there again. This demonstrates the extreme contamination that was produced in that great plain—so severe that the territory, even after being destroyed, has continued to be inhabited by demons until this day, as a cursed land:

"And Babylon, the glory of kingdoms, the beauty of the Chaldees' excellency, shall be as when God overthrew Sodom and Gomorrah.

It shall never be inhabited, neither shall it be dwelt in from generation to generation: neither shall the Arabian pitch tent there; neither shall the shepherds make their fold there.

But wild beasts of the desert shall lie there; and their houses shall be full of doleful creatures; and owls shall dwell there, and satyrs shall dance there" (Isaiah 13:19–21).

This teaches us a very important truth that we must consider in the practical aspects of Christian life. When considering the purchase or rental of a home, it would be wise to gain some knowledge of that location's history—and more importantly, to seek direction from God as to whether it should be inhabited.

It is not wise to speak lightly and say, "I'm a Christian; I can live anywhere—demons will have to flee."

"A prudent man foreseeth the evil, and hideth himself: but the simple pass on, and are punished" (Proverbs 22:3).

If evil spirits have a solid legal claim due to abominable practices previously carried out in that place, they will surely remain and become a malignant and disturbing influence over any Christian who foolishly insists on living in a place that is detestable to God, without submitting to divine law.

For this reason, it is imperative to receive direction from the Holy Spirit regarding the place where any family who honors the Lord Jesus Christ will dwell. Otherwise, the spiritual decline produced by cohabiting with demonic spirits will be so great that it will eventually bring some form of family destruction.

Some places can be purified, as shown in Leviticus 14:48. If the leprous spot did not persist, it was enough to replace the affected stones and scrape the walls to begin the purification process. However, in cases where the stain remained, the house had to be destroyed, and all its building materials cast into an unclean place. That is why it is crucial to seek the Spirit's guidance when purchasing or renting a home. It is unwise to act hastily in such matters.

This principle also applies when a congregation considers buying land or relocating to a new place of worship. God will not be pleased to see His people praising His name in a place that was once saturated with unclean practices. This could certainly result in serious delays in the progress of the work.

Another way a house can become defiled—perhaps the most widely used and promoted by the kingdom of darkness due to its subtlety—is found in Deuteronomy 7:26:

"Neither shalt thou bring an abomination into thine house, lest thou be a cursed thing like it: but thou shalt utterly detest it, and thou shalt utterly abhor it; for it is a cursed thing."

Unclean or abominable objects have become far more widespread today than in any previous generation. This is a highly effective strategy promoted by Satan to defile homes—especially the homes of believers. This method is often carried out almost silently, primarily through the ignorance of many of God's children regarding what constitutes an abominable object. This leads them to violate the command in Deuteronomy 7:26. Such violation—even if committed in ignorance—will not protect the household from the malign influences that are attracted through those things. For ignorance of the law does not exempt us from its consequences.

Therefore, it is necessary to be vigilant about every object that enters our homes. To counter this kind of attack, we must purposefully seek to understand what an unclean or abominable object is. Otherwise, we may unknowingly be surrounded by them.

An abominable object must be understood as anything that has had direct contact with or is associated with occultism, idolatry, witchcraft, divination, sorcery, pornography, or any other similar practice. The range of unclean items invented by Satan is vast, and many of them do not appear to be evil in nature. As we well know, he is the master of deception. In his strategy, he has chosen objects with an innocent appearance—such as stuffed animals, children's toys, decorative artwork, and many other things—which are tied to the filth of his abominations. These are cleverly disguised to deceive, especially the children of God, and to infiltrate their homes, establishing legal grounds for spiritual influence over those households.

Objects linked to occultism are those that have been involved in the worship of demons. Anything that has been used for such purposes becomes unclean. It could be a table, a blanket, a garment—any item used in those rituals. For this reason, we must be cautious with gifts that are given to us. This does not mean we must reject all gifts, but rather we must discern who is offering them.

In the epistle of Jude, it is written: "And others save with fear, pulling them out of the fire; hating even the garment spotted by the flesh" (Jude 1:23). Likewise, it is unwise to receive gifts from people we do not know—unless we have received specific direction from the Lord.

Another mistake made by some Christians is to bring home items they find on the street or purchase for extremely low prices from people living on the streets. Sometimes the excitement of finding what we need at a very low cost leads us into a trap of the devil. These items may be stolen, which makes them unclean, and in bringing them into our homes, we may be purchasing a curse at a cheap price.

Therefore, it is profitable for our spiritual life to consider these matters before bringing anything into our homes.

How have images of false gods found their way into so many homes? Any image of any demonic or idolatrous entity must be considered unclean. Likewise, the object on which the image is engraved, painted, or embroidered. Some homes even have altars built into their front walls bearing an image falsely named Mary. This creates legal grounds for demonic forces to exercise dominion over that household. It is not wise for a Christian to rent such a home, as they will be affected by the spirits claiming that territory.

In the same way, any image of the so-called Virgin Mary inside a house—whether in a picture, a canvas, a wall carving, or any other object within the perimeter of the home—grants legal access to the spiritual forces that hide behind those representations to cause harm.

I say "so-called Virgin Mary" because we know this image does not represent Mary, the mother of Jesus. She never intended to be worshiped or revered in a way that belongs only to the Lord Jesus. "His mother saith unto the servants, Whatsoever he saith unto you, do it" (John 2:5). Thus, when people build these images and worship them, they are actually being deceived by the evil spirits operating behind those idols.

Let me emphasize this point: the image of the so-called Virgin Mary is widely recognized among believers, which makes it easier to keep out of our homes. However, she is not the only spiritual entity being worshiped around the world; there are many others. And it is here that the deceptive strength of Satan lies: those images that are unfamiliar—because they belong to another culture, another country, or another era—have a greater capacity to infiltrate many homes unnoticed.

To achieve this, Satan has taken advantage of a tool that emerged in recent decades: television. For example, consider Amaterasu. Some may know who this entity is, but most believers in the Western hemisphere likely do not.

She is the sun goddess in Shintoism and the mythological ancestor of Japan's imperial family, according to that religion's beliefs. Also known as Ohiru-menomuchi-no-kami, her name means "the glorious goddess who shines in the heavens." She is one of the most important Shinto deities, worshiped as the goddess of the sky.

"The children gather wood, and the fathers kindle the fire, and the women knead their dough, to make cakes to the queen of heaven, and to pour out drink offerings unto other gods, that they may provoke me to anger" (Jeremiah 7:18).

This is the same spiritual entity that is called the Virgin Mary in Western cultures.

Surely, if a Christian were to have an image of the so-called Virgin Mary in their home, it would be scandalous. But the question is: what if they have an image of Amaterasu? Undoubtedly, it is the same thing—a spiritual structure of darkness. As Scripture says: "But I say, that the things which the Gentiles sacrifice, they sacrifice to devils, and not to God: and I would not that ye should have fellowship with devils" (1 Corinthians 10:20).

How do such images infiltrate Christian homes in Western nations? Television has played a major role in this, especially through Japanese anime, which has revived the names of many spiritually dark entities by portraying them as animated characters. This is the case with Naruto, where Amaterasu is mentioned among the characters.

Due to the widespread promotion through television, these characters gain global popularity, causing merchants to pay for the rights to use their images on various products. We see them on nearly everything made for children: school backpacks, notebooks, clothing, blankets, posters, coloring books, toys, and more. In some cases, they appear as physical figurines made of plastic or other materials.

Let us observe how cunning Satan is in his mission to bring abominable objects into homes and establish legal rights for demonic influence over them. First, he stirs individuals who are familiar with false gods and possess artistic skills to create animated series. Then, he brings this content to those who hold the tools of mass communication—television—with the purpose of making them famous worldwide. Afterward, he gives them commercial value, stirring entrepreneurs, both small and large, to stamp these images on their products for financial gain. Finally, these images and figures are physically brought into homes, especially into Christian homes.

Let us therefore be watchful regarding these matters. The absence of a Virgin Mary image in our homes does not necessarily mean we are free from every abominable idol. The enemy has been incredibly shrewd, disguising such idols in seemingly innocent images with the intent of defiling the purity that ought to be found in a Christian household.

We must be aware of what our children are watching on television—and even more so of what they are asking us to buy for them. Let us not be deceived by a natural parental instinct that seeks to satisfy every one of their requests. Rather, let us judge seriously the background of any character we consider allowing into our homes. Let us be sensitive to the inward direction of the Holy Spirit when we are about to purchase any item.

To give another example, let us consider the goddess Athena.

The goddess Athena holds a special place in the classical pantheon due to her role as the patroness of Athens and the protector of the Athenians. She is a spiritual entity who has been worshiped for generations. Her influence is not inferior to that of the gods who led the Israelites into failure. What I want to emphasize is the possibility that a Christian might have an image of this goddess in their home. One might ask: how could this be?

Let us consider how subtly the enemy operates. The animated series Saint Seiya (Knights of the Zodiac) widely publicized Greek mythology, including the goddess Athena. This series revives the image of a goddess who, according to the Word of God, is nothing more than a demonic entity, for there is only one true God. What is alarming is that a believer might unknowingly have such an image at home.

As previously mentioned, once a series becomes famous, its images acquire commercial value. Consequently, those images are physically reproduced as toys. Owning such a toy is equivalent to having an image of the goddess Athena in your house—there is no difference. Being declared unclean by the Word, it will bring a curse upon the home (Deuteronomy 7:26). Consider this seriously. If such an item is in your home, it may very well be the cause of significant family issues.

We easily identify the idolatrous system sold to us by Roman Catholicism, but we seldom recognize these other false gods, which can be subtly brought into many households. Here, we have only mentioned two examples, but there are many more. Every day, the enemy works tirelessly to revive the names of these entities and recreate them in physical form, thereby rekindling their influence over humanity. Let us be careful; let us not buy our children everything they ask for. Let us judge according to the Word of God.

Living in a rented room

Let us remember that the basic unit of governance is a house. Every house must have a person in authority—it is the foundational sphere of government. The geographical area under the authority of that person becomes their sphere of influence. Therefore, when living in a rented room—even if you are paying rent—you are under the influence of the authority of that household.

Within the church of the Lord, some brethren find themselves alone in terms of earthly family, and many do not own a home. Thus, it becomes necessary to rent a room if renting an entire house is financially unfeasible. It is important to note that a believer must discern wisely where they will live. This decision can seriously impact one's spiritual health. Living in a room within a household under a curse will gradually affect the believer, for they will be under the influence of a basic unit of governance—that is, a house.

If you need to rent a room, seek out a Christian family with a good testimony, one that pleases the Lord. This will protect you, and you will be blessed by the favor resting upon that household.

A resident under a curse

Another common situation is the reverse of what we just described. Some believers have a spare room and wish to rent it out. Curiously, something different happens in this scenario: if the person renting the room is under a curse, or if the room contains an unclean object, it will affect the blessing resting upon the entire house.

"But the children of Israel committed a trespass in the accursed thing: for Achan, the son of Carmi, the son of Zabdi, the son of Zerah, of the tribe of Judah, took of the accursed thing: and the anger of the Lord was kindled against the children of Israel" (Joshua 7:1).

Here is an important principle. In the case of Israel, it was a single man who took what was accursed; yet thirty-six men—who had nothing to do with it and were among the most chosen of Israel—lost their lives. Israel's function, from its sphere of government, was to conquer the city of Ai.

Achan's sin became exceedingly serious because of the sphere in which it occurred. Israel was advancing as a nation—this is, as a unit of government. Achan was part of this unit, and when he chose to sin, he failed to consider this principle. Therefore, as a part of the unit, by taking what was accursed, it was as though all of Israel had done it. This is the principle of the body: if one member suffers, the whole body is affected.

Based on the fact that the basic unit of government is a house, everything within that unit will affect the wellbeing of all who live there. The evil influence that may arise from the presence of an unclean object in one room will not remain confined to that space but will spread throughout the house, affecting all its inhabitants.

A person who is part of the household and is involved with unclean objects—by bringing them into the home—will bring with them the curse attached to those objects. It is essential that the head of the house be fully aware of who is living there and what they possess; otherwise, there will always be the possibility of contamination by evil.

If you rent out rooms in your home, you must carefully discern what kind of person will live there; otherwise, your household may be seriously affected. If there are family members in the house, aside from your children—such as uncles, cousins, etc.—it is important to know their conduct and their possessions.

Buying stolen goods

I would like to place particular emphasis on the matter of stolen items. You may think you do not have this habit, but by having even the smallest part in this chain, you become a participant in its curse.

"Then said he unto me, This is the curse that goeth forth over the face of the whole earth: for every one that stealeth shall be cut off as on this side according to it..."

(Zechariah 5:3)

You may ask how a Christian could be involved with stolen goods. There are many reasons, but I will mention only a couple.

Let us use common sense when it comes to the price of a product. If it is significantly below its normal cost, we ought to ask ourselves why. Often, behind an extremely cheap price, there is theft or some sort of injustice. Therefore, we should be suspicious when someone offers us something at a very low price.

For example, today it is no secret that the illegal market for cell phones is overflowing. Behind this, not only are there thefts, but even murders—many have lost their lives for their phones. From that moment on, such an object becomes unclean, for evil forces attach themselves to it. A Christian should not seek out vendors where the same phone costs half the price. Brethren, that is already suspicious. Do not make yourself a participant in the curse of the thief and the murderer for the sake of saving a few pesos.

There are legally authorized stores where you can buy phones—know where they come from. As much as possible, buy new from an established and authorized business.

In other cases, items are offered on the street, with an unknown origin. Let us not become accustomed to buying such things simply because they are cheap. The world is full of wickedness. Let us not participate in it.

"...Others save with fear, pulling them out of the fire; hating even the garment spotted by the flesh."

(Jude 1:23)

Evil can become so extreme that it even defiles the clothes a person wears.

It is not good to make a habit of buying second-hand clothing—especially from places where the origin is completely unknown. These garments may have been used to commit the worst atrocities and filth. If God clothes the grass of the field with glory—which today is and tomorrow is cast into the fire—how much more shall He clothe you, who has been made a child of God through Christ Jesus! You do not need to seek out second-hand clothes, particularly not ones with unknown origins, just because they are cheap.

How to identify demonic influence in a house

Just as in the Law there was a physical manifestation of evil in a house through leprosy, today there are also physical manifestations of demonic influences in a home, due to unclean objects.

In some cases, strange and unexplained noises are heard throughout the home—objects are heard moving without reason, strange things are seen, or there are supernatural manifestations. This is due to the presence of an evil entity, and it must have a foothold through some object, practice, or person dwelling in the home.

In other cases, persistent foul odors, continuous disorder, and filth reveal the presence of evil influences.

"Thou shalt have a paddle upon thy weapon; and it shall be, when thou wilt ease thyself abroad, thou shalt dig therewith, and shalt turn back and cover that which cometh from thee: For the Lord thy God walketh in the midst of thy camp, to deliver thee, and to give up thine enemies before thee; therefore shall thy camp be holy: that he see no unclean thing in thee, and turn away from thee."

(Deuteronomy 23:13–14)

If you do not feel peace and rest in your home, something is wrong. If you need to leave your house in order to feel calm, it is the result of an irregularity in your household. It is important to diligently investigate the reasons. Our home should be a place of peace and tranquility. The people who visit us should feel comfortable, breathing in the peace of the atmosphere where the Holy Spirit dwells. If this is not the case, something is happening; it is necessary to analyze the matter carefully.

These are some physical manifestations that may occur when a house is contaminated. However, there will be many more. May the Holy Spirit guide us in the discernment of these things.

How to purify a house

There are places that cannot be purified. The Bible mentions the plain of Sodom and Gomorrah. We are also told of Babylon:

"It shall never be inhabited, neither shall it be dwelt in from generation to generation: neither shall the Arabian pitch tent there; neither shall the shepherds make their fold there."

(Isaiah 13:20)

This is due to the great increase of wickedness in that place. Its contamination becomes so great that there is no purification for it.

The same applies to a house. We already mentioned the case of leprosy, in which it was necessary to tear down the house and throw its rubble outside.

Today, a house can reach this level of contamination. This results from abominable practices such as satanic rituals, cases of rape, bestiality, abuse and torture of children, among many other wicked deeds seen in this world.

In such cases, we should not dwell in these houses, for the multitude of their evils causes demons to claim that atmosphere as their own property.

In most cases, a house infected by demonic influences due to an unclean object can be purified. For this, it is necessary to identify the object or the cause that originated the contamination. If it is an object, it must be completely burned outside the house. Then, ask God for forgiveness for such disobedience, even if it was done in ignorance.

Invoke the blood of Christ, which cleanses us from all sin:

"...the blood of Jesus Christ his Son cleanseth us from all sin."

(1 John 1:7)

Afterward, exercise authority over the evil spirits that entered your house; cast them out in the name of the Lord Jesus Christ. If they have no foothold in the house, they will have to leave in the name of the Lord Jesus Christ.

If there are multiple objects, do the same with each one. It is important to be explicit so that the demons have nothing to cling to. In this way, you will be able to experience the deliverance of your house.

I have spoken briefly on these matters; however, I urge you to diligently inquire about the reality of this.

The marketplace is filled with objects related to false gods from various cultures—ancient, modern, indigenous, and others. Stay alert to every type of figure or image printed on what you buy or receive as a gift. Always ask God for discernment and remain sensitive to the voice of the Holy Spirit. And when you travel and visit other cultures, be cautious about what you bring into your home.

Chapter 7

Restitution, Key to Financial Blessing

A blessing is a spoken declaration made toward someone or something. It has the power to release good in a specific area. To bless is an act rooted in the principle of authority. Undoubtedly, the lesser is blessed by the greater: "And without all contradiction the less is blessed of the better" (Hebrews 7:7). Therefore, when an authority blesses their subordinates, that word is backed by God, by virtue of the authority they carry.

Based on this principle, as those who have authority in Christ, the Word of God commands us to bless and not to curse: "Bless them which persecute you: bless, and curse not" (Romans 12:14). Just as blessing becomes effective because it is spoken from a place of authority, so does cursing; however, we are not on this earth to curse, but to bless.

This spoken word is so binding that it cannot be revoked: "And Esau said unto his father, Hast thou but one blessing, my father? bless me, even me also, O my father. And Esau lifted up his voice, and wept" (Genesis 27:38). Once Isaac had spoken the blessing over Jacob, there was no way to undo it. A blessing spoken in authority is firm and irreversible.

Although blessing has the power to alter circumstances and open doors of opportunity, it is conditioned upon certain actions on the part of man: "Behold, I set before you this day a blessing and a curse" (Deuteronomy 11:26). Blessing requires a specific conduct and lifestyle from those who wish to partake of its benefits.

A blessing works in the direction of the area to which it has been declared—not necessarily in every area of the person's life. When we bless, it is important to be specific in declaring the area toward which the blessing is directed: "Even by the God of thy father, who shall help thee; and by the Almighty, who shall bless thee with blessings of heaven above, blessings of the deep that lieth under, blessings of the breasts, and of the womb" (Genesis 49:25).

When Jacob blessed his sons, he was specific regarding the areas in which they were to be blessed. This is important to understand, because for many people, the word "blessing" revolves solely around financial well-being. However, every area of our life needs to be blessed. There are those who are financially blessed but lack blessing in their family relationships. In the same way, it is possible to be blessed in one sphere of life and not in another.

This occurs because of the demands that blessing places as it seeks to permeate every part of who we are and what we do. We have a very firm foundation upon which to build: "Blessed be the God and Father of our Lord Jesus Christ, who hath blessed us with all spiritual blessings in heavenly places in Christ" (Ephesians 1:3).

We have been blessed with all spiritual blessings. Yet, this differs when it comes to subjective experience; for although it is true that we have already been blessed with every blessing, many believers do not yet see the manifestation of this in certain areas of their lives. This is due to the way our actions regulate the opening of the channel through which the blessing flows to us.

In this chapter, I want to focus on financial blessing. However, I would like to first define what it means to be financially blessed. Some interpret financial blessing as the accumulation of material wealth. However, there are many people—even Christians—for whom riches have led to destruction: "But they that will be rich fall into temptation and a snare, and into many foolish and hurtful lusts, which drown men in destruction and perdition" (1 Timothy 6:9).

This is not the blessing of God; for the blessing that comes from the Lord not only brings increase, but adds no sorrow with it: "The blessing of the Lord, it maketh rich, and he addeth no sorrow with it" (Proverbs

10:22). If the riches we acquire bring sorrow, then clearly, the blessing of God is not present among them.

Therefore, the goal is not to pursue riches, but rather, to seek God's blessing in our finances. A person who is financially blessed lacks nothing and has enough to share. When the blessing of God reigns over one's finances, it is possible to earn less than others, yet have more than enough, to give more, and to enjoy what one has: "Every man also to whom God hath given riches and wealth, and hath given him power to eat thereof, and to take his portion, and to rejoice in his labour; this is the gift of God" (Ecclesiastes 5:19).

I insist: the important thing is not to chase after money, but to ensure that the path of blessing is free of obstacles so it may reach us. This emphasis is crucial, for in many places today, greed and covetousness are disguised under the name of God's blessing.

However, in the lives of many of God's children, there is a noticeable lack of financial blessing—so much so that they are unable to cover even their basic needs, finding themselves in constant need of relying on credit. This is not part of the design of the Kingdom of Heaven for its citizens. It is common to see believers accept these conditions passively; yet it is not right to accept a model of life that is not backed by the Word of God.

The financial blessing that Job enjoyed was grounded on two pillars. First, his possessions were hedged about, so that Satan had no access to them. And second, God had declared a blessing upon the work of his hands: "Hast not thou made an hedge about him, and about his house, and about all that he hath on every side? thou hast blessed the work of his hands, and his substance is increased in the land" (Job 1:10).

Just like Job, the Christian should be hedged about, and the work of his hands should be saturated with God's blessing. But to be honest, this is not the experience of many believers today. It is very common to see Christians who work hard—and who have worked just as hard in different kinds of jobs—yet their financial situation never improves. They move to other cities in search of financial prosperity, but they do not find it. Even though they may be blessed in other areas, such as leadership, family, or health, their financial prosperity remains unchanged. Regardless of how many jobs they try or how hard they work, they continue to live in lack and are never able to help others—not even in the smallest way. Year after year, they endure the same hardship and scarcity.

This becomes a reproach to the Christian, providing the enemy an opportunity to shame him and expose him to ridicule; even the truth of the gospel becomes subject to criticism by unbelievers.

The first step in confronting this situation is to firmly and radically accept that this way of life is not part of God's design for His people. Many believers grow accustomed to this in a passive way. However, the solution is not to keep inventing new forms of work. What is needed is a serious examination of the Word of God.

If God has declared that we have already been blessed with all kinds of spiritual blessings, then without question, we have already been blessed—because God is not a man, that he should lie. The central issue, therefore, is not to ask God to bless us. His Word clearly states that we have already been blessed in Christ Jesus.

Wisdom lies in understanding what obstacle is hindering God's blessing. The main task, then, is to identify that obstacle. In this matter, the causes may vary; but here, I will focus on one possible reason behind this kind of issue.

Restitution: "Then it shall be, because he hath sinned, and is guilty, that he shall restore that which he took violently away, or the thing which he hath deceitfully gotten, or that which was delivered him to keep, or the lost thing which he found, or all that about which he hath sworn falsely; he shall even restore it in the principal, and shall add the fifth part more thereto, and give it unto him to whom it appertaineth, in the day of his trespass offering" (Leviticus 6:4–5).

This principle is rarely taught today, yet it is the very reason why the blessing is blocked in the lives of many Christians. It is commonly believed that once a person comes to Christ, they must completely forget their past. And while this is true in a certain sense, there are matters that should not be forgotten—especially those that involve wrongs and unresolved debts. The believer is called by the Spirit to make restitution: "And Zacchaeus stood, and said unto the Lord; Behold, Lord, the half of my goods I give to the poor; and if I have taken any thing from any man by false accusation, I restore him fourfold" (Luke 19:8).

After Zacchaeus had an encounter with the Lord Jesus, he felt the need to restore what he had taken—going so far as to offer four times the amount. And while it is not a legal requirement to return fourfold as Zacchaeus did, there is a biblical principle to add a fifth part to what was stolen or defrauded (Leviticus 6:5).

Therefore, in every matter in which we have defrauded or wronged someone, it is necessary to restore it and add at least a fifth part—even if the wrongdoing occurred before coming to Christ. Zacchaeus had likely stolen from many, and all of it before he came to know the Lord. Likewise, anyone who turns to the Lord is called to return what was stolen and make restitution for the harm done.

Some try to justify their lack of restitution by claiming that they have already been justified in Christ. However, it is essential to understand what we have been justified from when we receive Christ. Our justification in Christ concerns the record of decrees that was against us (Colossians 2:14). In other words, we are justified from our debt toward God—a debt that was impossible for us to pay. This debt placed us in a state of injustice before God, but Christ chose to pay it in full. Thus, we are justified in Christ Jesus from all that we owed to the Kingdom of God. However, debts owed to men still remain—and these must be made right.

For example, if someone argues with their spouse and, in the heat of the moment, speaks a hurtful word, and later realizes they were wrong, the matter cannot be resolved simply by asking forgiveness from God. Though the divine commandment was certainly violated and the Lord was indeed offended, He is not the only one offended. Therefore, while one must ask God for forgiveness for breaking His command, there is still a human debt to settle. One cannot presume that everything is resolved just by asking God's forgiveness— there is also a person who was hurt and awaits restitution. A wise Christian will understand this, and after seeking God's forgiveness, will approach their spouse, acknowledge their offense, and seek their forgiveness as well.

This is precisely what happens with justification in Christ: every time someone is wronged, it stems from a violation of divine law. The sacrifice of Christ settles man's debt with God—a debt caused by transgression of His law. However, in cases where a third party is affected by the sin, restitution becomes necessary.

Although the Christian has been justified before God, he is also called to be just toward his fellow man. The Lord Jesus said, "For I say unto you, That except your righteousness shall exceed the righteousness of the scribes and Pharisees, ye shall in no case enter into the kingdom of heaven" (Matthew 5:20). Therefore, there is a form of righteousness that man must develop in relation to others. Let us look at two passages to better understand this.

In Romans 3:10, the Word says: "As it is written, There is none righteous, no, not one." However, in Matthew 1:19, it says that Joseph was a just man. Based on this, we might ask: is there anyone righteous, or not? The answer is: yes and no. There is no one righteous before God—we have all become sinners, violators of His law, that is, transgressors. This left man in a condition of unfitness for fulfilling God's purpose. Yet, there have been men who were just in their dealings with others.

This does not mean that a person who is just with others has become justified before God—not at all. Human acts of justice do not erase transgressions against divine law. For this reason, justification before God is not attained by works (Galatians 2:16), for there are no human works capable of removing transgressions. However, the blood of our Lord Jesus Christ was able to do it: "Much more then, being now justified by his blood, we shall be saved from wrath through him" (Romans 5:9). And this, freely given: "For by grace are ye saved through faith; and that not of yourselves: it is the gift of God" (Ephesians 2:8).

Joseph, though a just man, was not saved by this righteousness, for it was a righteousness he developed toward others. To be justified according to the demands of divine justice, he too needed the blood of Christ.

Although the blood of the Lord Jesus positions us on the foundation of righteousness before God, this does not cancel the need to develop righteousness toward our fellow man. Without this, the Christian may hinder the blessing that has already been declared over his life.

Let us now apply this principle to the matter of restitution and how the lack thereof can block financial blessing.

I insist: we must not limit ourselves to the moment we gave our lives to the Lord; rather, we must recall every instance in which, before coming to Christ, we stole or defrauded someone, so that we might make restitution.

Though this is not something often heard, it could very well be the key that unlocks financial blessing for many Christians who have tried everything to break free from continual lack.

Every time a debt is incurred, a commitment to pay is established. Once that commitment is broken, and no new agreement is made, the individual enters a state of injustice. This state will persist until the debt is paid—regardless of whether the person has surrendered their life to the Lord. The continued presence of the debt reveals the ongoing state of injustice.

To clarify once again: this is not a state of injustice before God. It is not something that directly compromises one's salvation, but it does affect one's blessing in this life. As long as the debt remains unpaid, the blessing will remain stagnant in heavenly places due to the argument of injustice operating within the believer.

One delicate situation in this regard is money earned through labor—that is, withholding wages from someone who has worked for them: "Thou shalt not defraud thy neighbour, neither rob him: the wages of him that is hired shall not abide with thee all night until the morning" (Leviticus 19:13). The Lord places great value on the money a person earns through their labor. When this money is withheld by an employer, it constitutes a serious financial injustice, because the laborer lives off his wages. By doing so, he is being deprived of his livelihood.

Perhaps we will not find Christians who currently practice such things; yet, it is possible that they did so repeatedly before coming to the Lord. Even if such a person has been justified before God, they still owe a debt to their neighbor. As long as the wronged person has not received restitution, this remains as a mark that cries out against the believer, affecting their blessing. If someone is truly saved, they will naturally seek to repair the damage they caused—not out of legalistic obligation, but out of love and justice. God does not demand the impossible, but He does require a sincere willingness and concrete action toward making things right. One may set up a payment plan, ask for forgiveness, offer alternative compensation or assistance, and so on.

This is important to understand. Many Christians are faithful in tithing, give offerings as they are able, work diligently, and manage their spending with discipline; yet, their financial provision remains limited, and they often find themselves in great need. If this is your case, it would be wise to reflect on this matter, as your situation might be rooted in this very principle.

In the same way, this applies to borrowed money. Many people are careless in this matter: they borrow money and later forget to repay it. It is also important to consider who the money is owed to, for although any unpaid debt places the Christian in a state of injustice, there are certain debts that demand greater attention. For example, withholding payment owed to a poor person or a needy widow: "Ye shall not afflict any widow, or fatherless child" (Exodus 22:22). When unpaid debts affect individuals in these categories, the level of injustice increases significantly.

In other cases, items or property are obtained on credit, and the payment is delayed indefinitely— sometimes never being fulfilled. Even if the person did this before knowing Christ, now that they belong to Him, they are called to make restitution, and to add an amount to what is restored. This will break the arguments used by the forces of darkness to block their blessing in the heavenly places.

Let us remember that the issue is not asking God to bless us, for He has already blessed us in Christ with all spiritual blessings in heavenly places (Ephesians 1:3). Note two key truths:

First: We have been blessed with every kind of blessing—including financial blessing, which refers to our work and all that we undertake in financial matters.

Second: The blessing has been declared in heavenly places. Therefore, it needs to descend to us. If years go by and we do not experience this blessing, without a doubt it is because there is a legal system of divine law that is holding it back in the heavenly realms. One reason may be neglecting the principle of restitution.

A very important issue to consider here is the financial responsibility one has toward their children after the fragmentation of a home. As is common, the mother retains custody of the children. This often results in neglect, and in extreme cases, total abandonment of the father's financial responsibilities toward his children. This becomes an injustice that cries out against the man: "But if any provide not for his own, and specially for those of his own house, he hath denied the faith, and is worse than an infidel" (1 Timothy 5:8). Knowing Christ does not absolve a man from this responsibility; rather, it urges him to face the matter with seriousness and erase the injustice through restitution. This could very well be a major reason for significant financial blockage. A man is obligated to provide financially for his children while they are still minors—even if they do not live with him. Withholding this provision places him in a state of injustice, and on that basis, the enemy has legal grounds to restrain his financial blessing.

It is important to look back and remember the times we borrowed money and never repaid it, or the times something was given to us on credit—be it a product, item, or property—and the payment was never fulfilled. Or perhaps we left someone unpaid for work they had done. All these matters constitute legal grounds that can compromise a Christian's financial blessing.

In light of this, we must be practical—otherwise, the issue will remain unresolved until death, and we will remain bound for life to something we can be free from.

The first step is to make a list of every situation in which we entered into a financial obligation and never fulfilled it. For this, it is essential to dedicate time to prayer, for there may be things we have completely forgotten. We need the illumination of the Holy Spirit to reveal every unresolved matter still standing in the heavenly places against us—especially those we may no longer remember.

Once we have clarity on who we have wronged or defrauded, we must establish a plan for restitution. Otherwise, it will never happen. Do not fall into the trap of thinking, "I'll pay that debt when I have extra money." That moment will never come. It is necessary to develop a financial plan in order to restore what was lost to those who were affected by our actions.

Each person will design their plan according to their financial capacity. For example, you might set aside a certain percentage of your income for the purpose of restitution.

It is important to set priorities in terms of who should be restored first. The most sensible approach is to begin with the most serious offenses. By "most serious," I do not mean the largest monetary amounts, but rather the situations involving the highest degree of injustice— such as failure to support one's children or unpaid wages, among others.

When a Christian's financial blessing has been hindered, the restitution process can be difficult because income is often limited. However, firmness in the decision to act on this principle will be honored by God. He will open doors and help you accomplish it. It is also important to add an extra portion to what is restored. We can apply the biblical principle revealed in Leviticus 6:5, which instructs us to add a fifth part—that is, twenty percent—to what was taken or defrauded.

Whenever possible, it is also important to ask forgiveness from the person who was wronged.

Without a doubt, things will begin to change. Every blockage that darkness has maintained in the heavenly realms will have to be released. The financial system will have to shift: new opportunities will spontaneously arise, and we will see the reality of our blessing in Christ Jesus saturating every work we undertake. "And whatsoever he doeth shall prosper" (Psalm 1:3).

There is a situation in which the process of restitution becomes particularly complex. Although I addressed this earlier in Chapter Five, I will mention it again here: the absence of the person who was wronged.

This may be due to the possibility that the person has moved to an unknown location and cannot be found, or perhaps the individual has passed away.

The first step is to genuinely exhaust all human means to locate that person. If there is no possibility of finding them—as in the case of death—the next step is to seek out a descendant of the wronged individual, such as a son or a grandson, and make restitution to them.

If it is still impossible to find any descendant of the person who was wronged, we must bring the amount owed as an offering to the Lord Jesus, presenting it before a church authority, and make a confession of the offense in their presence. That authority should then pray for the believer so that the restitution may be accepted and the offense remitted at the cross of Calvary: "Whose soever sins ye remit, they are remitted unto them; and whose soever sins ye retain, they are retained" (John 20:23).

This must be done for each unresolved case where the person or their descendants cannot be found. Every offense must be confessed individually; every matter must be resolved individually, because each offense was committed individually.

Chapter 8
The Laying On of Hands

Hebrews 6:2 speaks of the laying on of hands as one of the foundational doctrines of Christ—that is, as a basic teaching in the Christian life. In this chapter, we will broadly discuss the importance of understanding how this practice functions in the life of the believer, so that we may apply the laying on of hands with understanding, according to biblical foundations.

The laying on of hands serves two fundamental purposes:

1. First, connectivity, meaning the establishment of a connection between two people.
2. Second, transference, which is the capacity to transmit part of the essence or content of one being to another.

This principle is used throughout the entire Bible. It was practiced by the patriarchs:

"And Israel stretched out his right hand, and laid it upon Ephraim's head, who was the younger, and his left hand upon Manasseh's head, guiding his hands wittingly; for Manasseh was the firstborn" (Genesis 48:14).

It was also used under the Law:

"And the elders of the congregation shall lay their hands upon the head of the bullock before the Lord: and the bullock shall be killed before the Lord" (Leviticus 4:15).

And the early Church used this principle as well:

"Whom they set before the apostles: and when they had prayed, they laid their hands on them" (Acts 6:6).

In all these cases, the purpose remains the same: to unify in order to transfer. Human beings have the God-given ability to transfer—and they do so through their hands.

As I mentioned in Chapter Two, every spiritual principle can be used either by the light or by darkness. The fact that it is a principle makes it immutable and applicable in both domains. Therefore, not only the good within a person can be transferred, but also the evil.

In occult practices, this principle is used to transfer spiritual forces to subordinates. Let us examine more closely how this practice was used in Scripture:

"And Joshua the son of Nun was full of the spirit of wisdom; for Moses had laid his hands upon him" (Deuteronomy 34:9).

This verse reveals the function of the laying on of hands—Joshua was filled with the spirit of wisdom because Moses had laid his hands on him. This means the spirit of wisdom that dwelt in Moses was imparted to Joshua. But for this to occur, a connection was needed—and this connection was established by the laying on of hands.

"And Aaron shall lay both his hands upon the head of the live goat, and confess over him all the iniquities of the children of Israel, and all their transgressions in all their sins, putting them upon the head of the goat" (Leviticus 16:21).

This matter deserves careful attention. One of the most important practices in the covenant made with the Hebrew nation was the Day of Atonement. This practice allowed for the covering of the people's sins, iniquities, and transgressions each year. But in order for this to happen, the principle of the laying on of hands had to be used. Aaron, acting as high priest and representative of the people, would lay both his hands on the animal. This would immediately establish a connection. Then came a confession—of both sins and iniquities and transgressions—resulting in the transfer of those sins onto the head of the animal.

Therefore, it is not only spirit that can be transferred through the laying on of hands, but also sins, iniquities, and transgressions. For this reason, Paul exhorts Timothy not to partake in other people's sins by laying hands hastily:

"Lay hands suddenly on no man, neither be partaker of other men's sins: keep thyself pure" (1 Timothy 5:22).

This shows us that it is possible to transfer sin. If it were not, the atonement in Israel would not have been possible. Yet it was a true and God-ordained practice. Indeed, the goat was sent into the wilderness carrying the people's sins, iniquities, and transgressions. If this had not been truly possible, God would not have instituted such a command. The fact that it was done every year proves its reality. This practice was founded upon the principle of the laying on of hands.

As I have stated before, principles remain immutable.

Even today, this principle is just as real as it was for them. Just as it was real that the animal carried all that evil, it is also real that a person can bear another's evil through the laying on of hands. Not only sins, as Paul mentions to Timothy, but also iniquity and rebellion— which are even more serious matters.

"And the elders of the congregation shall lay their hands upon the head of the bullock before the Lord: and the bullock shall be killed before the Lord" (Leviticus 4:15).

Here we see the same principle applied to sin. But in this case, it involved a bullock. This was done when a collective sin had been committed—that is, when the entire congregation had fallen into the same sin. In such cases, the elders of the congregation were to lay their hands on the bullock and then sacrifice it.

Throughout the entire worship system of the old covenant, we see the practice of laying on of hands as a principle of connection and transference. Without this principle, atonement would not have been possible—an act that symbolized the sacrifice of Christ, the Lamb of God who takes away the sin of the world.

Therefore, this is not a light matter nor something to be taken casually. Every time hands are laid on someone, an immediate connection is established with the purpose of transferring something. It is irresponsible to go around laying hands on people carelessly and without discernment.

This practice was also used by the Lord Jesus:

"And he could there do no mighty work, save that he laid his hands upon a few sick folk, and healed them" (Mark 6:5).

He also laid His hands on children to bless them:

"And he took them up in his arms, put his hands upon them, and blessed them" (Mark 10:16).

The apostles also made use of this principle:

"And when Simon saw that through laying on of the apostles' hands the Holy Ghost was given, he offered them money" (Acts 8:18).

Notice that Simon saw that the Holy Ghost was given through the laying on of the apostles' hands. Thus, the principle of laying on of hands was used by the early church to transfer the Holy Spirit, who already rested upon the apostles.

The same principle from the Old Covenant is being applied. The apostles laid their hands on the new believers, creating a connection, and then the Spirit of the Lord that dwelled in the apostles was transferred to the new convert:

"Then laid they their hands on them, and they received the Holy Ghost" (Acts 8:17).

"And Ananias went his way, and entered into the house; and putting his hands on him said, Brother Saul, the Lord, even Jesus, that appeared unto thee in the way as thou camest, hath sent me, that thou mightest receive thy sight, and be filled with the Holy Ghost" (Acts 9:17).

"And when Paul had laid his hands upon them, the Holy Ghost came on them; and they spake with tongues, and prophesied" (Acts 19:6).

What I want to emphasize through all of this is the necessity of understanding this principle, because it is not good for the church when believers go around laying hands on everyone. It is important to understand this and to use it properly. When used correctly, this practice will surely be a blessing to the church. But if it is misused, many believers may be affected.

We must be watchful and ensure that this is done responsibly. It is not wise to lay hands on others without a basic understanding of what is taking place, as this can cause spiritual contamination in the life of the believer. It is important that the person laying hands be an experienced authority with a good testimony before the congregation. Otherwise, it is best to avoid allowing others to lay hands on us.

The laying on of hands is a practice closely related to the Kingdom of God; this makes it dependent on the principle of authority, which is the very foundation upon which the Kingdom is established. If we speak of laying on of hands, we must also speak of authority; one cannot be discussed without the other. Not everyone has the right to lay hands on just anyone; it must be done in order—and that order is a line of authority.

Every time we see the laying on of hands in Scripture, we see it within a line of authority. Moses laid his hands on Joshua to transfer from his spirit in authority. When Aaron laid hands on the scapegoat, he did so in his role as priestly authority, representing the people. Similarly, when the congregation of Israel sinned, it was the elders who laid hands on the bullock, for they were the representatives of authority among the people.

In the book of Acts, this is shown even more explicitly:

"Now when the apostles which were at Jerusalem heard that Samaria had received the word of God, they sent unto them Peter and John: who, when they were come down, prayed for them, that they might receive the Holy Ghost: (For as yet he was fallen upon none of them: only they were baptized in the name of the Lord Jesus.) Then laid they their hands on them, and they received the Holy Ghost" (Acts 8:14–17).

I find it striking that, after Philip had accomplished such a great work in Samaria, the presence of the apostles was still necessary for the new converts to receive the Holy Ghost.

Couldn't Philip pray for them and lay hands on them so they would receive the Holy Ghost?

The answer is: No!

Why not? Because the laying on of hands is done based on authority; and in this particular case, the laying on of hands was for the purpose of imparting the Holy Ghost. Therefore, the presence of the highest authorities in the church was required—namely, the apostles—"and God hath set some in the church, first apostles" (1 Corinthians 12:28). On this occasion, Philip did not have the ministerial authority for such an act. While he was able to lay hands on people so they would be healed of their diseases, he did not possess the authority to lay hands for them to receive the Holy Ghost.

This is an important distinction to make: even if someone has authority to lay hands in one ministerial area, that doesn't necessarily mean they have authority in another.

Hands should not be laid upon someone in authority to bless them, because it is the authority who must lay hands to impart blessing. This is not to say one should not pray for their pastor; this is not about prayer. The laying on of hands is tied to the principle of authority, and must flow within that principle.

Through the laying on of hands by spiritual authorities—such as parents, grandparents, pastors, apostles—spiritual gifts can be received. "Wherefore I put thee in remembrance that thou stir up the gift of God, which is in thee by the putting on of my hands" (2 Timothy 1:6). It is evident that Timothy received gifts from God through the laying on of Paul's hands, who was his authority.

1 Timothy 4:14, in the Contemporary English Version, renders it in a very particular way: "Use the gift you were given when the group of church leaders laid their hands on you. The Holy Spirit told them what to

do." Indeed, many spiritual abilities can be received through the laying on of hands, as long as it is done according to the principles of the Kingdom of God—namely, under divine order and spiritual authority.

Parents can transfer blessing to their children through the laying on of hands: "And Israel stretched out his right hand, and laid it upon Ephraim's head, who was the younger, and his left hand upon Manasseh's head, guiding his hands wittingly; for Manasseh was the firstborn" (Genesis 48:14).

Pastors can transfer gifts to the church through the laying on of hands: "Neglect not the gift that is in thee, which was given thee by prophecy, with the laying on of the hands of the presbytery" (1 Timothy 4:14).

It must always be done within a line of authority. All of us have a position of authority, and depending on the purpose of the laying on of hands, we may be permitted to do it. When this principle is used correctly, it is a great blessing to the body of Christ.

It is important to understand what we have to impart. Peter said, "Such as I have give I thee". One cannot impart what one does not have, even if they are in a position of authority. We must examine ourselves before laying on hands. For example, a father is indeed in a position to impart blessing to his children by the laying on of hands. However, that father must be filled with blessing—otherwise, what will he be transmitting?

A person filled with greed, lust, or envy cannot impart anything other than what is within them.

Therefore, when a connection is established through the laying on of hands, it is what resides within the person that will be imparted. The same is true within a congregation: if the pastor does not live a life founded in holiness, then what he imparts to the people will be the substance of his own heart. That is why it is wise to examine ourselves before laying on hands, lest we do harm instead of good.

Chapter 9
The Principle of Authority

"And Joshua, and all Israel with him, took Achan the son of Zerah, and the silver, and the garment, and the wedge of gold, and his sons, and his daughters, and his oxen, and his asses, and his sheep, and his tent, and all that he had: and they brought them unto the valley of Achor. And Joshua said, Why hast thou troubled us? the Lord shall trouble thee this day. And all Israel stoned him with stones, and burned them with fire, after they had stoned them with stones" (Joshua 7:24–25).

"For as in Adam all die, even so in Christ shall all be made alive" (1 Corinthians 15:22).

"Let it rest on the head of Joab, and on all his father's house" (2 Samuel 3:29).

This is a principle of great importance in the Word of God, for it is the very structure upon which all of creation is built. Unlike Satan, who establishes his kingdom upon rebellion, the kingdom of God is founded on authority and submission.

All of us, in one way or another, are both under authority and in authority. And the greater the number of people under one's care, the greater the accountability before God: "But he that knew not, and did commit things worthy of stripes, shall be beaten with few stripes.

For unto whomsoever much is given, of him shall be much required: and to whom men have committed much, of him they will ask the more" (Luke 12:48). Depending on the position of authority we hold, we may be empowered either to do great good—or to fall into great evil.

Every time a human being sins, they do so from a place of authority—whether small or as great as Adam's. The Word of God says: "In Adam all die." This statement is astounding, for none of us had been born at the time, yet when Adam chose to disobey, we were all dying together with him that very day. Perhaps even Adam himself did not grasp the full weight of the damage he was causing. This happens when we are unaware of the authority we've been given. Adam was dragging millions of human beings into death—perhaps without even realizing it.

The damage that can be caused is proportional to the level of authority one holds. However, authority is not given to harm, but rather to provide protection: "Thou art the anointed cherub that covereth; and I have set thee so: thou wast upon the holy mountain of God; thou hast walked up and down in the midst of the stones of fire" (Ezekiel 28:14). But when authority fails, it destroys everything under its care: "And his tail drew the third part of the stars of heaven, and did cast them to the earth: and the dragon stood before the woman which was ready to be delivered, for to devour her child as soon as it was born" (Revelation 12:4).

Therefore, we must not desire authority lightly if we do not understand the responsibility that comes with it.

The case of Achan is a clear example of how a person in authority can bring destruction upon those they are meant to protect. This is a deeply serious matter, and if we were to look at it with the weight it deserves, we would think twice before failing.

When Achan was stoned, he was not stoned alone. His sons, his daughters, his oxen, his donkeys— everything he owned was stoned along with him. Even the poor animals suffered the consequence of his foolishness. Why? Because of his position of authority. Every time a person sins, they do so from a position of authority, and everything under them will be affected by that sin.

When King David sinned by numbering the people, not only was he rebuked, but the people also suffered punishment. A man cannot claim to love his children while committing adultery. What he is actually doing is condemning them to a generational curse.

Every time a man sins, he does so within a sphere of authority; and as a result, not only will he be affected, but so will everything under his care—including animals. When Adam disobeyed, he was not the only one to suffer death as a consequence. Every living creature on the planet was affected. Even the trees experience death, because they were all placed under Adam's authority: "And God blessed them, and God said unto them, Be fruitful, and multiply, and replenish the earth, and subdue it: and have dominion over the fish of the sea, and over the fowl of the air, and over every living thing that moveth upon the earth" (Genesis 1:28).

What has God placed under your authority? The success of everything under your care depends on the decisions you make. Every time a father gives himself over to pornography, he is condemning his wife and children to be plundered by unclean spirits. It is no wonder that under such circumstances, children may suffer abuse or fall into bondage to fornication. All of this is the result of fallen authority.

The most precious treasure the Kingdom of God possesses in this world is the human soul. The trust that God has placed in man is immense, granting him the ability to reproduce. To welcome into the arms of a home the most helpless and innocent being on earth—a baby— is an act of great confidence that the Kingdom of God extends to mankind. Yet, on many occasions, we betray that trust and harm the most precious possession the Lord has entrusted to us.

One of the greatest wounds a child can suffer is the fragmentation of the home. According to psychology, the brain damage experienced by a child in such circumstances is comparable to what a soldier endures in war. Many men condemn their children to this fate by pursuing adultery.

This is what Achan did: he condemned his family to death by doing what he had been told not to do. The same was true of Adam: he condemned all of creation to death by doing what he was commanded not to do. What has God entrusted to you? What has He told you not to do, yet you continue in it? It is crucial that we reflect on this and consider seriously how many lives may be affected if we choose the path of disobedience.

When Elisha's servant took what he should not have from the Syrian, he did not consider the consequences: "But Gehazi, the servant of Elisha the man of God, said, Behold, my master hath spared Naaman this Syrian, in not receiving at his hands that which he brought: but, as the Lord liveth, I will run after him, and take somewhat of him" (2 Kings 5:20). As a result, he condemned not only his children but all his descendants to the disease of leprosy: "The leprosy therefore of

Naaman shall cleave unto thee, and unto thy seed for ever" (2 Kings 5:27).

Therefore, every human being holds a position of authority—whether small or great. Even someone who believes they have no one and nothing still carries within them a future lineage, even if they haven't yet had children. One day they likely will, and their children will have children, and so on. All those descendants are within them. Thus, every action we take today will affect an entire future generation.

To whom much is given, much shall be required. One of the highest honors God grants some of His children is to shepherd His flock. However, those in such a position must know that they will be held to a higher standard. Every action they take will affect many. Satan understands this principle well—he knows he can bring down many by taking down just one man. "I will smite the shepherd, and the sheep of the flock shall be scattered abroad" (Matthew 26:31). Many congregations have suffered irreparable harm because their pastor fell. But just as much harm has come through fallen authority, so also has great blessing abounded through those who have stood firm in obedience.

"For as in Adam all die, even so in Christ shall all be made alive" (1 Corinthians 15:22). Just as we were dying on the day Adam chose to disobey, so we were being made alive on the day Christ rose from the dead—even though in both cases, we had not yet been born.

Because one man in authority chose to obey, seven others were spared—and not only seven, but all of humanity in him. "By faith Noah, being warned of God of things not seen as yet, moved with fear, prepared an ark to the saving of his house; by the which he condemned the world, and became heir of the righteousness which is by faith" (Hebrews 11:7). In the same way, when an authority learns to walk in obedience to the Lord, entire congregations are blessed and lifted to new spiritual levels.

"Lift up your heads, O ye gates; and be ye lift up, ye everlasting doors; and the King of glory shall come in" (Psalm 24:7). Brothers and sisters, the King of Glory enters through the gates—He does not climb over fences. And those gates are the authorities. If we, as those in authority, do not open the gates to the King of Glory, our entire government will be affected. "And unto the angel of the church of the Laodiceans write... Behold, I stand at the door, and knock" (Revelation 3:14, 20). The Lord calls upon the authorities to enter a territory. An entire nation could be transformed if its leaders would confess the iniquities of their people and open the door to the King of Glory.

An authority does not only have the responsibility, but also the legal capacity, to protect those under their care. "And it was so, when the days of their feasting were gone about, that Job sent and sanctified them, and rose up early in the morning, and offered burnt offerings according to the number of them all" (Job 1:5). A person can be forgiven and sanctified through the intervention of their authority. I speak now to those of us who are fathers: Are we offering sacrifices and sanctifying our children? Or are we condemning them through our actions? Will we follow the example of Achan, who brought death upon his family, or the example of Noah, who led his family through the floodwaters?

We do not know much about the lives of Noah's children; we know little about their righteousness. But what we do know is that because of Noah's righteousness, his entire family was saved. These are the consequences of an authority who has learned to obey.

Chapter 10
The Spoken Word

"For verily I say unto you, That whosoever shall say unto this mountain, Be thou removed, and be thou cast into the sea; and shall not doubt in his heart, but shall believe that those things which he saith shall come to pass; he shall have whatsoever he saith" (Mark 11:23).

Here we find one of the greatest challenges the Lord ever placed before His disciples. And it all begins with something simple: the Lord was hungry, and seeing a leafy fig tree, He went to find fruit on it. Yet He found nothing. Then came the word: "No man eat fruit of thee hereafter for ever." To the disciples' astonishment, the fig tree withered from the roots. They were surprised—but what the Lord said next would leave them even more amazed. And I believe that even now, centuries later, it still astonishes us.

How is it possible to speak to a mountain and see it move? Someone once asked me, "Has anyone ever actually moved a mountain by speaking to it?" To which I replied, "Not that I know of—but I do know of a man who said, 'Sun, stand thou still upon Gibeon; and thou, Moon, in the valley of Ajalon,' and the unimaginable happened: this planet, with a diameter of 12,742 kilometers, came to a halt."

Scientifically, they say this would be impossible. The Earth spins at about 1,700 kilometers per hour; if it were to stop suddenly, everything on it would be flung into chaos—much like slamming the brakes in a speeding car. And yet, it happened. How? I don't know. I only know that it did.

This led me to a question: which is easier—to move a mountain, or to stop the entire Earth? Honestly, from a human perspective, the former seems easier than the latter.

I say this because many Christians struggle to believe that the Lord was referring to a literal mountain. We often argue, "He was talking about a problem or a difficulty." And while that interpretation may apply in some cases, the fact remains: the Lord stood before an actual mountain, pointed to it, and said to His disciples:

"For verily I say unto you, That whosoever shall say unto this mountain, Be thou removed, and be thou cast into the sea; and shall not doubt in his heart, but shall believe that those things which he saith shall come to pass; he shall have whatsoever he saith."

For those who cannot accept that the Lord was referring to a literal mountain, I ask: which is more difficult—moving a mountain or stopping the entire Earth? While Scripture does not record anyone moving a mountain with their words, it does testify of a man who caused the entire planet to stand still with his words.

Therefore, the issue is not whether it's a mountain or the whole Earth—the real issue is whether the human heart has the capacity to believe in the Word of God. There is a deep connection between the heart and the mouth.

"For out of the abundance of the heart the mouth speaketh" (Matthew 12:34).

"But those things which proceed out of the mouth come forth from the heart; and they defile the man" (Matthew 15:18).

"But what saith it? The word is nigh thee, even in thy mouth, and in thy heart: that is, the word of faith, which we preach" (Romans 10:8).

"For with the heart man believeth unto righteousness; and with the mouth confession is made unto salvation" (Romans 10:10).

We could cite many more verses on this subject, but the main point here is the necessity of speaking or confessing what is believed in the heart. In Mark 11:23, the heart is mentioned once, but the verb "to say" appears three times, giving greater emphasis to the act of speaking. There is a manifestation of faith in speaking, because a verbal testimony is required for the power of the word to be released. It is not enough for it to remain in the heart.

The heart is structured in such a sealed way that only God can truly know it. But when it comes to expressing power, it is necessary to declare through words what is believed in the heart, as a testimony to all spiritual beings involved—since they cannot read the heart of man. They will only know what is within by what comes out of his mouth.

If we want to know what fills a Christian's heart, all we need to do is sit and listen to them speak. A Christian who speaks of everything except the Word of God will hardly experience the power that God's Word can unleash in the life of one who confesses it. It does no good for a believer to constantly speak complaints about their health, their pastor, their fellow believers, or their neighbors. Such speech reveals what truly fills their heart.

"Let the words of my mouth, and the meditation of my heart, be acceptable in thy sight, O Lord, my strength, and my redeemer" (Psalm 19:14).

Are the words of our mouth pleasing to God? It would do us well to reflect on this.

Although we are often unaware of the Lord's presence, He is always listening to what we say—from morning until night. "Thou knowest my downsitting and mine uprising, thou understandest my thought afar off" (Psalm 139:2). The Lord hears us at all times. Are we truly aware of this? If we are, we will not speak behind someone's back words we are not willing to say to their face.

Are the words of our mouth pleasing to the Lord? Let us meditate on this for a moment. Of all the words that have come out of our mouth today, how many have been pleasing to the Lord? How many have been indifferent to Him? And how many have offended Him? The answer to this personal examination will determine our effectiveness when it comes to moving mountains.

The truth is, our words will not be pleasing to the Lord unless the meditation of our heart is pleasing to Him first. A Christian who has not trained their heart to meditate on the Word of God day and night is far from seeing a manifestation of God's power in their life.

It is dangerous to allow the meditation of our heart to be filled with the cares of this life instead of with God's Word. Perhaps this is one of the main reasons why men who move mountains are so rare in our time.

While it is true that we need to plan and prepare for life in this world, that does not mean our hearts should be filled with its anxieties. The desire for a better job, a college degree, a house, a car, and many other earthly pursuits may gradually saturate the heart of a believer until their meditation is no longer pleasing to the Lord.

Under such conditions, it is very unlikely that one will have glorious experiences with God.

It is troubling when a Christian knows more about politics, mathematics, movies, football, or other kinds of knowledge than they do about the Word of God. Our primary ambition in life should be to be filled with the Word of God in our hearts. "Let the word of Christ dwell in you richly" (Colossians 3:16). If you agree with me in wanting to see the manifestation of the power of God's Word in our lives, then we must seriously consider what we are filled with.

What occupies the majority of our thoughts? That is what is filling our heart.

In order to step into the challenge the Lord gave His disciples—when He told them they could even move a mountain—it is essential for the Word of God to saturate our hearts, to become the dominant thought within us. If we reach that point, we are on the right path in our pursuit of the manifestation of God's glory.

Starting from that foundation, we come to our second action.

Once our heart is saturated with the Word of God, it must be released. And the way to release it is through our mouth. Truly, there is no greater power in the universe than this; in fact, the universe itself was created by the Word of God. "Through faith we understand that the worlds were framed by the word of God" (Hebrews 11:3). The problem is that many Christians think they are the ones who must provide the strength and power to move the mountain—and this leads them to unbelief. It was not Joshua who made the earth stop. Rather, Joshua's heart was saturated with the Word, and that Word was released through his mouth, providing the power necessary to halt the planet's rotation for nearly an entire day. Therefore, we should not be concerned with how great the challenge before us is, for with the Word of God, nothing is impossible.

There are countless galaxies and innumerable worlds in the universe, and all of them were created by the Word of God. Every living being that moves in this world was created by the Word—and it is that same Word that brings salvation to us. "For with the heart man believeth unto righteousness; and with the mouth confession is made unto salvation" (Romans 10:10). What is believed? The Word of God. And what is confessed? The Word of God.

When a man's heart is filled with the Word of God, and he releases it through his mouth, salvation is produced. And the same process applies to any other kind of miracle. Therefore, our concern should not be the size of the giant standing before us. In reality, what killed Goliath was not David's sling, but the Word of God. When that young man declared the Word that filled his heart, the giant fell. "Thou comest to me with a sword, and with a spear, and with a shield: but I come to thee in the name of the Lord of hosts, the God of the armies of Israel, whom thou hast defied" (1 Samuel 17:45).

Although physically the giant was struck down by the sling, spiritually, he had already been pierced by the sword of the Word of God.

There is great importance in releasing the Word that is in our heart. We can be filled to overflowing with it, but if we do not speak, the Word cannot do its work. In Mark 11:23, the verb "to say" is emphasized—because although the Word is powerful in itself, it must be spoken. And when that happens, the same power that brought the universe into existence is released to accomplish that for which it was sent.

It is wonderful to know that the Word of God has been entrusted to us. "And take the helmet of salvation, and the sword of the Spirit, which is the word of God" (Ephesians 6:17). What does it mean that the Word has been entrusted to us? It means that the Word of God does not only come from the mouth of God—it can also proceed from the mouth of those to whom it has been entrusted. This is a privilege exclusive to the people of

God. "But unto the wicked God saith, What hast thou to do to declare my statutes, or that thou shouldest take my covenant in thy mouth?" (Psalm 50:16).

Therefore, the use of the Word of God is a privilege given to the saints. And that is truly glorious! The most honorable thing we can do is to honor this trust by seeking to fill ourselves with this glorious Word above all else.

A Christian whose heart is saturated with the Word of God is a believer who has a supernatural weapon in their mouth. All it takes is for that Word to be released, and extraordinary things begin to happen. No matter how adverse the situation may be—simply release the Word. Even if the sea rages and the night is dark, let the Word come out of your mouth and command the storm to be still; surely, there will be a great calm.

There is no reason whatsoever to doubt the Word of God. If the Word brought the universe into existence, how much more can it create everything we need on our journey through life. Let us not be overcome by doubt; let us not close our mouths out of fear of being put to shame. If we do, we will only be granting the enemy victory over our lives.

There is a well-known saying: "Silence gives consent." In the spiritual realm, this is absolutely true: "If a woman also vow a vow unto the Lord, and bind herself by a bond, being in her father's house in her youth; and her father hear her vow, and her bond wherewith she hath bound her soul, and her father shall hold his peace at her: then all her vows shall stand, and every bond wherewith she hath bound her soul shall stand" (Numbers 30:3–4).

When we remain silent in the face of something, we are passively accepting it. But not everything is meant to be accepted—there are situations that must be confronted with the Word of God.

The Word of God is truth, and when it is released, powerful things happen. No matter how great your challenge may be—declare the Word over it. Brothers and sisters, the Lord Jesus Christ, who is the Word, has given us authority to proclaim it—even over the elements of creation. God said to Moses, "Speak ye unto the rock" (Numbers 20:8), and the Lord told His disciples they could speak to the mountain. This means we can speak to mountains, to rocks, to the city where we live, to the sea, to rivers, to animals—to anything we can believe in our hearts. Absolutely all of creation is subject to the Word of God, even inanimate objects.

The weapon God has entrusted to us and placed in our mouths is exceedingly powerful. Let us not remain silent before the enemy—speak the Word! With such a weapon, it is unthinkable for a Christian to keep letting the devil steal from them. Do not allow the evil one to destroy your family or rob you of your job. Open your mouth against him, and let the Word of God execute judgment against all your enemies. And you—rest in full assurance of faith. For so it shall be.

Printed in Dunstable, United Kingdom